SCHOOL LIBRARIAN'S
CAREER PLANNER

*ALA Editions purchases fund advocacy, awareness,
and accreditation programs for library professionals worldwide.*

SCHOOL LIBRARIAN'S CAREER PLANNER

Hilda K. Weisburg

An imprint of the American Library Association
CHICAGO 2013

Hilda K. Weisburg retired as library media specialist at Morristown High School in Morristown, New Jersey, and has taught graduate courses at William Paterson University and Rutgers University. A past president of the New Jersey Association of School Librarians (AASL), she is the association's delegate to AASL's Affiliate Assembly to which she has served as chair. Currently, she is on the ALA Literacy Committee and AASL's Retiree Task Force. She has served on numerous other AASL committees as well. Along with Ruth Toor, she has written fourteen books for library media specialists, including two for ALA Editions, *Being Indispensable: A School Librarian's Guide to Becoming an Invaluable Leader* (2011) and *New on the Job: A School Library Media Specialist's Guide to Success* (2007). She is now the publisher and sole editor of the bimonthly electronic newsletter *School Librarian's Workshop*, which has been in publication since 1980. Weisburg has given presentations at AASL and state library media conferences and given staff development workshops in many locations.

© 2013 by Hilda K. Weisburg. Any claim of copyright is subject to applicable limitations and exceptions, such as rights of fair use and library copying pursuant to Sections 107 and 108 of the U.S. Copyright Act. No copyright is claimed for content in the public domain, such as works of the U.S. government.

Printed in the United States of America

17 16 15 14 13   5 4 3 2 1

Extensive effort has gone into ensuring the reliability of the information in this book; however, the publisher makes no warranty, express or implied, with respect to the material contained herein.

ISBNs: 978–0-8389-1178-5 (paper); 978-0-8389-9642-3 (PDF); 978-0-8389-9643-0 (ePub); 978-0-8389-9644-7 (Kindle). For more information on digital formats, visit the ALA Store at alastore.ala.org and select eEditions.

Library of Congress Cataloging-in-Publication Data
Weisburg, Hilda K., 1942–
  School librarian's career planner / Hilda K. Weisburg.
     pages cm
  Includes bibliographical references and index.
  ISBN 978-0-8389-1178-5
  1. School librarians—Education. 2. Library science—Vocational guidance. 3. School librarians—United States—Handbooks, manuals, etc. 4. Career
     development. I. Title.
  Z682.4.S34W45 2013
  027.8—dc23   2012040942

Cover design by Casey Bayer. Image ©Lightspring/Shutterstock, Inc.
Text design in the Warnock Pro and Centennial typefaces by Scribe Inc. Composition by Scribe Inc.

♾ This paper meets the requirements of ANSI/NISO Z39.48–1992 (Permanence of Paper).

*To Ruth Toor, my coauthor and friend for thirty-five years.
It was a very strange experience doing this solo. I missed you.*

and

*To Jay Toor, our publisher for almost thirty years. I thank you for your
generosity and kindness. I will never forget the gift you gave me.*

CONTENTS

Introduction ix

1   Getting Your First Job in the Field 1
2   Acing the Interview 13
3   Selecting the *Right* Job 25
4   Mastering the Learning Curve 37
5   Growing Your Career 47
6   Polishing Your Skills 63
7   Moving Outwards 79
8   Taking Charge 93
9   Moving On 111

Index 123

INTRODUCTION

*"It's good to have an end to journey towards,
but it's the journey that matters in the end."*

This quote has been attributed to several sources, but its message is one that should guide school librarians as they embark on their career. Some may plan to find a position and stay with it to the end. Others may from the first want to be supervisors or administrators. All, in one way or another, will find that life events require changes to be made to original plans. It is best to keep options in mind from the very beginning. Using the *School Librarian's Career Planner* as a guide, you will always have an option B—and often an option C to allow you to skillfully weather whatever comes your way.

School librarianship is a career requiring the ability to develop relationships, build leadership skills, and be a lifelong learner. The path to the profession varies widely. Some start as teachers and become interested through that route. A few have always wanted to be a school librarian and seek the degree immediately after graduating from college. Others volunteer in their child's school library and realize how much they love working in that environment, and there are those who have had careers in the corporate world or any number of jobs outside of education but for one reason or another become attracted to the profession.

The possible career paths for school librarians is an area largely ignored both in the literature and in library school. The common belief is that one gets a degree, finds a job, hopefully is awarded tenure, and then remains in that district until retirement. Yet life rarely works like that. Those who are most successful have learned they can make choices and plan strategically to create a career that is within their control and infinitely rewarding.

School librarianship is frequently a second career, but even those who come to it from teaching and are familiar with the educational system are not fully aware of the possibilities. Library school rarely covers the multifaceted aspects of how school librarians can successfully carve out a unique niche within the educational community. Given the current economic conditions, new practitioners, now more than ever, need to be astute in how they

- Present themselves
- Learn the workings of the school and district while still demonstrating expertise
- Develop the skills needed to assume various leadership positions (both official and unofficial)
- Prepare for changes that still keep them active whether it is the result of staff cuts or a personal decision
- Plan for a retirement that is as rewarding as their work world

The *School Librarian's Career Planner* guides readers from finding the right first job to having a rewarding retirement. Starting with resume writing through the interview, the first steps and possible pitfalls are outlined as candidates are shown how to be alert throughout the interview process. Even while promoting themselves as the best applicant, they must be listening carefully to what is being said—and not said—so they can accurately determine whether the situation is the right one for them. Unlike a classroom teacher, a school librarian's job can vary tremendously from one district to another, and sometimes from one building to another.

Once school librarians are in the job, it is up to them to continue to evolve professionally, be aware of developments in pedagogy and technology, integrate the two, and incorporate their new knowledge and understanding into the fabric of the school. Their leadership must be evident. As they develop management skills, in addition to other abilities, they are frequently given more responsibilities such as chairing important committees and even some administrative opportunities.

The wise school librarians are always prepared for change, including moving on from a job they had loved. Even the best of them can get caught up in a district-wide elimination of positions. Work conditions can alter when a new administrator takes the helm. In the former case, there is no option. In the latter, it is important to realize when it is time to leave. The key is for them to know where to go next, recognizing that they still have choices, and can continue to contribute to the profession and their own well-being.

Along the way, part-time work in other types of libraries can expand expertise and, in some cases, lead to a change in career direction. Eventually, every career winds down and it becomes time to retire. After so many years in the forefront of what is new in technology and education, those post-work years need not be a slow slide into decline. With the same planning that marked the rest of their career, librarians can continue to contribute and find personal fulfillment. Once a librarian, always a librarian.

1
GETTING YOUR FIRST JOB IN THE FIELD

You are seeing the light at the end of the tunnel. With your coursework almost finished and your degree imminent, it is time to get started on your career by landing a great, if not perfect, job. Most of you have learned by now that to attain long-term results, you need to plan, which requires gathering information and determining which choices will get you where you want to go. Reacting to events leaves you at the mercy of whatever currents come your way. Become the architect of your life and design it so that you attain your goals and have the rewarding career you dreamed of when you first chose to enter this field. Put those skills to work as you search for your first school library position.

You have advantages and disadvantages as you begin your search. Being inexperienced is both a positive and a negative. On the plus side, you will be starting off at the bottom of the salary scale, making you a bargain for a school district which may have been paying the guide maximum to the librarian you will be replacing. The drawback is your lack of background. You may struggle with interview questions; you have no track record in the field; and, if you get the job, the administrators may see this as an opportunity to assign duties and responsibilities they would not have given to the outgoing librarian. In a tough economy, the latter is more true than ever as staff cuts often mean covering several schools, not having clerical staff (if there had been such help), and taking on teaching classes. In some cases, the person you are replacing left because of these changes.

You will have to weigh these demands against your need and desire to have a job in the field. While recognizing that there are likely to be many candidates for any open position, you do not want to lock yourself into an untenable situation that will cause you to lose your enthusiasm for your career choice and struggle to complete the school year. By being aware of options and resources, and being clear as to your choices, just as with selecting your library school, you can find a job that will be a good fit.

SEARCHING FOR YOUR FIRST JOB

Even before graduation there are several steps that should be undertaken. First and foremost is to be sure you have completed all the requirements for getting certified in your state. Since what is listed on the state's website is not always clear, it is fortunate that your library school, whether traditional or online, will be able to help you with the process. Although you will not have the actual document until you have completed your course work, it is helpful to let potential employers know that it is in the works. States can be very slow in issuing licenses, but human resource departments are well aware of what the timeline is likely to be.

The best place to see what jobs are out there is your library school's placement office. If you are attending a traditional face-to-face program, you probably have already been looking at the bulletin board listing open positions and so have a good idea of the number of openings and what is being sought by districts in your state. A good online program provides most of the same resources with an electronic bulletin board for openings.

Most state library associations have a page on their website listing job openings. If your state is one that has a separate organization for school librarians, check both associations' websites. If you have not done so already, become a member and join the electronic discussion list most have. Job openings are often announced there first, sometimes by the librarian who is leaving the position.

Newspapers are another potential source. School districts tend to be traditional in their approach and most still advertise openings in local papers. Statewide papers are best. Even before you begin your search, you should find out which ones are most likely to carry job listings in education.

Another resource is the ALA JobLIST, and you need not be a member to have access to it. You can subscribe at http://ala.informz.net/ala/profile.asp?fid=1494. It appears weekly in your in-box. In addition to listing openings, it is a treasure trove of advice for job seekers. Articles cover the full range of what applicants need to know. You might find links to resume writing or how to prepare for interviews. Each week brings new information that will give you the help you need to find a job and land it. For more information about the ALA JobLIST and what it offers, go to http://joblist.ala.org/jobseekerfeatures.cfm.

Be prepared to apply for jobs that would not be your first or even second choice. In a tight market, you need to be flexible. However, you do not want to take a position that would make you miserable for even one year. Building experience so that you can be a better candidate in a district where you do want to work is good, but be careful that the situation you accept is at least workable for one year. Resigning mid-year will make your next search that much harder.

Successful Search Strategies

1. Do you know the requirements for certification in your state? Will you have completed them by graduation?
2. What services are offered by your library school's placement office? Which ones can you use right now?
3. Have you joined your state association(s)? Are you on the electronic discussion list? Have you checked out job openings on their website?
4. Which newspapers in your state/county list openings in education?

SOCIAL MEDIA: THE GOOD AND BAD

The online world of social networking starts in middle school, and sharing personal information becomes so habit-forming, many do not stop to consider the electronic trail they are leaving. Well before you actively begin your job search, you need to be sure that you have nothing damaging posted. It is amazing to human resource personnel how unaware applicants can be about what their online persona reveals. Hopefully, you are wise enough to have abandoned any e-mail addresses that are inappropriate. (A possibly apocryphal story alleges that one candidate stated she could be reached at partygirl@aol.com. Definitely not the right image.)

A good start is to Google yourself and see what results. The human resource department will do this, so it is best to know what they will find. You may be surprised at what is out there about you. If you are going to be working in a school you do not want a Facebook page that has pictures of you drinking or that has inappropriate posts. You may have to take down photos and even your page.

Blog posts are another potential hazard. If you have your own blog, you know your topics and the content. Again, depending on what you shared, it may be necessary to close this out. Some posts you made on other blogs might also show up in your search. Do what you can to have any deleted that you would not want administrators (or your future students) to see.

On the other hand, social networking can be very valuable. You can create a blog that puts you in a very positive light, perhaps structuring it around what you are learning in library school. Focus on the big questions that courses are raising in your mind. Discuss your belief that a school librarian teaches students *how* (not *what*) to think, guides them into understanding how to build new knowledge, and how to become ethical digital citizens.

As part of your course work, or perhaps you have done so on your own, you learned how to create a web page. While this is to teach you how to do one for your library, you can also create a personal one to showcase your abilities and interests. Your blog can be a part of it. Its design will be a good indicator to a prospective employer of your technological expertise.

Another good use of social networks is to join professional ones such as LinkedIn (www.linkedin.com) and Plaxo (www.plaxo.com). Go on both. Put up your profile and invite people you know to join your network. Ask them to write recommendations for you which are available to others who search for you or your skill set. You will soon see names of potential connections. Ask any who will be of potential help to accept your invitation to become part of your network. Post any new accomplishments and skills so that those who have included you in their network are kept abreast of your professional development.

Socially Speaking

1. What was the result of your Google search on yourself?
2. Were you surprised? Is there anything that needs to be cleaned up?
3. What are some topics you can address on a blog?
4. What will you put on your profile for LinkedIn and/or Plaxo?

WRITING YOUR RESUME

Whether or not school librarianship is your first career, you need to create a resume that shows you are a candidate worth considering. Ruth Toor and I addressed the process in *New on the Job: A School Library Media Specialist's Guide to Success*, but the advice bears repeating along with additional information about how to construct this key piece in your job search.[1] The Internet has so many resume templates and samples both free and for a fee that you can quickly become overwhelmed by the sites. Don't spend too much time here. You just need to get an understanding of what your resume might look like.

Pick two or three sites, preferably with samples. You will quickly see that while there are variations in formatting, most are similar in organizational structure. All resumes must have your complete contact information on top, clearly readable. Whether you box and/or shade this, or use a hard underline, is up to you. Be aware, if you are going to be e-mailing your resume, to keep formatting very simple. It may not come through otherwise.

Even if you are sure that you will not be sending your resume via e-mail, choose an easily readable font. Times New Roman, Arial, Verdana, or Tahoma are best. Script fonts and informal looks such as Comic Sans are not to be used. Whatever font you select, stay with it throughout.

Print your resume on any reasonable weight paper in white (or ivory). It is not necessary to purchase "resume paper." Do not get "cute." Fancy paper with "school-theme" borders should not be used, even if you are applying for an elementary position. You want your resume to have a professional look.

Your name, address, and contact information including e-mail address *must* be at the top of the page. Some like to put their name in a larger font size or use bold typeface. Just be sure that all of this is easily readable.

If this is your first job, *Education* typically comes first, followed by *Experience* (more on this later). For those who have had other careers, the order is normally reversed. However, before listing the information in these two areas, you need to consider what leads into it. Stating your *Objective* tends to be the most common but is generally rather boring and trite and undoubtedly barely looked at by either the human resources department or administrators. Typically it reads, "To obtain a challenging position as a school librarian," or more creatively, "To obtain a school library position where I can impact the lives of students." Of course, that is what you want. On the other hand, it is so obvious that it is a waste of space to offer it.

You will get more attention if you begin with a *Profile* or a *Summary*. For this you can use some adjectives to describe yourself (e.g., "a tech-savvy school librarian with the skills to inspire others with my passion for twenty-first-century learning . . ."). Here is where you can highlight your strongest qualities. You can either present it in two or three statements (not full sentences) or as a bulleted list. Keep it to not more than four bullets, and begin each with a descriptive, dynamic word or phrase (e.g., "resourceful," "skilled communicator," "proven leader"). In the balance of your resume, you give examples that show how these qualities were gained on the job (or in your leadership activities in graduate school).

Determining what to include as *Experience* is as challenging for those with previous multiple careers as it is for those who went straight from college to library school. Your experiences need to be relevant to the position or they are inconsequential. Consider the skills you will need on the job. You have become aware of many of them during your course work. Show how your previous jobs have honed them and will enable you to bring a greater dimension of service as a school librarian. If you had contact with customers, either in person or as part of a help desk, what were you able to do that gave them what they needed? What leadership expertise did you develop? Did you give trainings? All of these can show that you will be an asset even with little or no experience in school librarianship.

Look to your volunteer work to give added breadth to your resume. Have you been involved in scouting? Taught classes in your church or temple? Any of these can be listed under *Education-Related Experience.* You can use these activities to demonstrate your ability to connect with students.

Additional information can make a difference between you and an equally worthy candidate. Definitely list all library and education associations to which you belong. You can safely use **NEA** rather than the National Education Association, but do spell out **ALA** and **AASL**. Administrators are not likely to be familiar with them. Being a member shows your commitment to your chosen profession. If you serve on a committee for one of these organizations, list it. You will be demonstrating your interest in and understanding of the larger issues facing education and school librarianship. Also include any honors you received and, if by some chance you had the opportunity to write an article that was published, include that as well.

At one time, resumes would indicate the computer operating systems and software programs with which you were proficient. Today, that is a given, but you should include specialized skills such as web design and understanding of Web 2.0 tools, including open source.

You will probably be asked to submit the names of references. Few places want you to send the references themselves. They would rather contact the people themselves, knowing it will produce more honest results. Speak to those you want to list and make certain they are prepared to give you a positive recommendation—without reservations. If you are not sure they can do this, go elsewhere.

Do not overlook the resources of your school's career center, whether online or traditional. Check to see if and when they offer workshops on resume writing. Some provide one-on-one critiques by school librarians and others who are involved in the hiring process. Length is often a concern. Some say a resume should not be over one page, but you can have two pages. If you do, be sure it is not one-and-a-quarter pages, which looks peculiar. Also, put your last name and the page number on the top of the second sheet in case the pages get separated. This is also important if you are e-mailing your resume.

If you are sending your resume via e-mail, save it as plain text because formatting can get garbled when sent into cyberspace. Read the employer's directions carefully. Many places do not want attachments, fearing viruses. In that case you will be doing a cut-and-paste into your e-mail (below your cover letter). Send it first to yourself to see how it looks and make any necessary changes before e-mailing it to the appropriate administrator or human resources department.

One final source of help and advice is your own personal network. If you have classmates or know others who have recently gotten jobs as a school librarian, have them look over your resume. Ask to see theirs. You may want (with their permission) to use some of their wording and ideas. Do get someone to proofread your resume. It is amazing how many resumes reach administrators' desks with spelling and other errors.

> **Perfecting Your Resume**
> 1. What will you highlight in your *Profile* or *Summary*?
> 2. Which of your job experiences can you "tweak" to demonstrate how it will make your library program better?
> 3. What volunteer work can you use to show "education-related" experience?
> 4. What "extras" can you list?
> 5. Whom will you ask for recommendations? Do they represent a range of your experiences and abilities?
> 6. What resume resources are offered by your college's career center?

RESEARCHING A PROSPECTIVE EMPLOYER

Unless you live in or close to the town where you plan to apply for a position, you should do serious research on the educational community and its administrators. Sites such as www.greatschools.org let you know which ones are considered to be among the best, but a lot depends on how they are doing the ranking. Very often, districts with students from diverse backgrounds are rated low, yet they may be challenging, open to new ideas, and filled with a sense of commitment and purpose.

Many states have developed a system of reporting how schools are doing so that parents (and prospective newcomers to a town) can determine how a district measures up to those with a similar student population. These, too, need to be analyzed carefully. Test scores tend to be the basis for the rating. You will not be surprised to see that high-income locations are invariably at the top of the list. Magnet schools, specializing in a specific content area such as technology or the arts, also are usually among those ranking near the top.

These ratings give you background but should not be a deciding factor. You will be drawing on them to ask questions during your interview to get a better idea of how administrators see their school and what their vision is for taking it to the next level. A high-ranking district can be very complacent. While it will embrace the "next thing" in technology, it might not wish to explore changes in teaching methodology. If that is the school's culture, many teachers will have the same attitude. Depending on how you feel about bringing change, this situation might not be a good fit for you. On the other hand, a district that has done poorly on tests and other indicators may now have new administrators who are looking for exciting approaches to motivate students (and faculty) and will be open to your ideas.

Your next step is the district and school websites. You may find a mission statement here. Most are fairly cookie-cutter and do not tell you much, but check out the links and see what you can find. For example, the Morris School District in New Jersey, under "District Information," states, "The Morris School District is a unifying social force and a source of tremendous pride in our community. In our classrooms and on our playgrounds children of every race, religion, and economic background come together to learn with and from each other."[2] It continues with other information on the number of schools, grade levels, and average class size. But those two opening sentences tell you much more that is significant. You immediately know that the district is diverse, and by implication has a strong commitment to multiculturalism. The term *pride* is indicative of how it views itself and its place in the community. *Pride* used in this context is a word rarely seen on most school websites, and its presence gives you a sense of the underlying culture.

Check on what the student body is doing. Websites often tell you about athletic and academic teams, special awards, and community service projects. Not only does this give you a sense of familiarity with what is going on in the district, you also learn where it puts its emphasis. Obviously, you want to see what is on the library's page. Some are absolutely brilliant. You immediately know it is central to everything happening in the school. Others have a few statements about hours and borrowing privileges with a few pictures of library happenings. Exploring several of these will help you quickly realize how well you can probably evaluate the quality of a program by what is posted on the website.

Next research the administrators. Human resource departments will Google you, and you need to do the same with the administration. Using the school and district websites, see what you can find out about the superintendent of schools and the principal. You may locate a page listing a workshop they have presented, giving you a clue as to their special area of expertise. Very probably they are on LinkedIn (www.linkedin.com), which will provide you with their past employment history. If the administrator has a common name such as Patrick Brown, add "principal" or "superintendent" to your search term. It will greatly reduce the number of false hits. The information you glean will help you prepare for your interview—and indicate whether or not you want to work in that district and school.

> **Ready with Research**
> 1. Research your local school district. Did what you find fit with what you know? Did you learn something about the administrators?
> 2. Do the same with two or three districts in which you are interested. Which one seems like the best fit for you? Why?
> 3. Compare your district's website with the others that you researched. Which gave you the most information? Which seems like an inviting place to work (and send your children)?
> 4. Which of those districts' school library websites seem to have the best program? If possible, visit them and see how reality compares with the online "picture."

COVER LETTERS—PRINT AND ONLINE

The cover letter introduces you to prospective employers. You have only one opportunity to make a first impression. While this letter follows a standard format in overall structure, the contents can set you apart from other applicants and make people want to read your resume.

The opening paragraph states where and how you learned of the job opening. After that initial statement, applicants typically say something like, "I will be graduating in May and believe my background and interest make me an excellent candidate for the position." While not bad, it falls into the cookie-cutter category. Administrators receive so many like that, they barely read it. A far better approach is to draw on the research you did on the district and say, "I am applying because the Blank School seems to focus on a whole child approach which is aligned with my own educational philosophy." No matter what the district is doing, you can invariably tie your background and interests to it, making the reader immediately recognize that you are not just churning out cover letters.

The second section is where you sell yourself in one or two paragraphs. You should not be repeating what is in your resume, but you can highlight key features about yourself. For example, you might be able to state, "In addition to my qualifications as a school librarian, I enjoy integrating technology into whatever I am doing, which can be seen throughout my resume." Perhaps your strength lies in your communication skills. In that case you could say, "I believe strongly in community outreach which includes faculty and staff as well as parents, using my experiences in web design and e-mail newsletters."

In other words, while you do have to briefly indicate you have the basics required for the job, show you are bringing something extra. At the high school level, you could even include interest in coaching or other cocurricular activities. This can be a particularly good selling point if it is in an area that is important to the district. If you want to promote several of your skills, you can use bullet points. Do not go overboard here. You are including your resume.

The final paragraph is another place to stand out from the crowd. Usually it thanks the reader for his or her time and includes the hope for an interview. It might also indicate contact information, even though that is on the resume, but state "I can best be reached at . . . ," giving your e-mail address, cell phone, or whatever is your *primary* means of communication. Do not waste the space. Give administrators a reason to want to call you for an interview. Say something like, "I hope you will give me the opportunity to discuss with you how the school library program can be instrumental in achieving district goals." It would help if you could refer to a goal from the district's website.

As with your resume, if you are e-mailing, find out whether the district wants your cover letter as an attachment or sent within the body of your message. In the latter case, you still must begin with a proper salutation and have a business closing. Do *not* type your letter directly into the e-mail. Create a document on your word processing program and then cut and paste it into the e-mail to be sure there are no missing words, misspellings, or other grammatical errors. If you are sending the cover letter as an attachment, keep the font simple. Again, complex formatting does not always come through at the other end.

Note that in an e-mail cover letter, your signature block is below your name while in hard copy it is placed at the top of the page. Make sure your subject line is clear and to the point, such as "Elementary Library Position, Name of School." Be sure to indicate within your cover letter if you are including your resume within the e-mail, following the district's guidelines. Remember at all times that you are presenting yourself as a professional. This is not a place for using emoticons.

When sending your cover letter and resume via snail mail (and priority mailing is a better idea), make sure the paper matches. If you chose special paper for your resume, use it also for your cover letter. Whether done online or hard copy, keep your cover letter brief. You are sending a resume. All you are doing in the letter is creating the interest that will have your prospective employer consider looking at the resume and feel positively disposed to it. Finally, make certain you have the correct spelling of the names of the recipients—and the school—to which you are applying.

If you are concerned about your cover letter, remember to check out your school's career center. Just as with resume writing, it should provide you with samples you can use. Someone there might even be available to review what you have written.

> **Covering the Bases**
> 1. Choose a district where you would like to work and compose a sentence for your first paragraph that would explain why you would like to work there and what makes you eminently qualified for this potential position.
> 2. What strengths will you highlight in your second paragraph? Try a few samples and ask one or two friends or colleagues to critique them.
> 3. Using that same district, which goal could you address in your closing paragraph?

KEY IDEAS

- Make sure you have completed all the paperwork for your certification before job hunting, or that it's in progress awaiting your graduation.
- Start you job search with your college's placement office.
- Check the website of your state's library association(s) for openings.
- Know which newspapers in your area carry education job listings.
- Subscribe to the ALA JobLIST.
- Do your best to clean up any "inappropriate" content you may have posted on social media sites.
- Join professional social media sites.
- Use your school's career center to learn how to craft a professional resume.
- Scrupulously follow employer directions for submitting resumes.
- Consult your professional network (fellow students and colleagues in the field) to have them review your resume and critique it.
- Research the district to which you are applying to develop an understanding of its composition, academics, and so on.
- Write a cover letter that shows you are familiar with the district, and use it to promote one or two of your strongest points.

NOTES

1. Ruth Toor and Hilda K. Weisburg, *New on the Job: A School Library Media Specialist's Guide to Success* (Chicago: American Library Association, 2007).
2. Morris School District (New Jersey), www.morrisschooldistrict.org.

2
ACING THE INTERVIEW

Although business texts invariably observe that interviews are not good indicators of whether someone will be a good or bad hire, the education community as well as the corporate world still rely on them heavily in making their decisions. While every job hunter works diligently to be called in for one, it is important to remember that an interview is not the goal. It is merely the first step in the process of reaching it.

Because the interview is so important, you must prepare for it as you would the most significant test in one of your hardest courses. Rehearsing and coaching are vital to being successful. By acquiring as much information as possible about the district, the school, and the position, you will go into the meeting with confidence which will make you an attractive candidate.

PREPARING FOR AN INTERVIEW

When the call you have been waiting and hoping for finally comes, you must be ready for it. After you and the secretary have set the time, date, and location for the interview, do not just say thank you and hang up. See if you can get some advance information. Generally, you will be seeing the principal, but others may be present, and being forewarned is far better than being surprised. Ask whether any additional administrators, such as a supervisor, or the librarian will be there.

Check whether there is any special procedure for visitors, including parking or which entrance to use. In these days of higher precautions, once the school day is underway you often have to use a specific door and press a button to gain entrance. Larger schools typically have a security desk where you must sign in and receive some sort of I.D. to show you have been cleared for entry.

Use the lead time until your scheduled appointment wisely. Refer back to your research on the district and its administrative personnel. Google any who will be part of the interview that you did not look up earlier. Reacquaint yourself with the district's website and that of the library. Find out more about the community served by the school. While you are not likely to use this information during the interview, it will give you background that will add to your comfort level during a stressful situation.

If you have not done so as yet, purchase your interview outfit. For men, a suit and tie is always preferable, but a sports jacket can work. Casual is out, no matter what the typical dress is in that school. Obviously, sneakers and other such footwear are not to be worn. A suit (not dowdy, but not flashy either) is an excellent choice for a woman. The skirt should be long enough to cover the knees when sitting. Slim is fine; tight is not. If you are unaccustomed to wearing skirts, choose a pants suit. You do not want to be worrying about your clothing while trying to concentrate on the questions. Low-heeled shoes are a good idea as you may be doing some walking. Avoid long, dangling earrings or bracelets that might catch or clink. Neither you nor the interviewer will be pleased with the distraction.

Do a dry run to the location, preferably at the same time of day as your scheduled interview. You do not want to worry about getting lost or stuck in traffic on the actual day. Even with this preparation, leave plenty of time to reach your destination. You need to time to relax, and collect your thoughts (and use the restroom), before greeting the administrator.

The real key to success is practicing in advance. Lawyers never go into an important case without this preparation, and you need to be as ready as possible before walking in to what is a major step in your career. Going over the opening handshake, making sure that anything you are carrying is on your left side, leaving your right hand free is a start. You might want to have a few possible greetings, such as "Mr. Smith, I am so happy to meet you." Be sure you have pronounced the name correctly. If there is a potential for not getting it correct, make sure to ask the secretary when you set up the interview.

The most important part of practicing is anticipating possible questions and planning how you will answer them. Anticipate both softball and hardball ones. If you are not prepared, even something as simple as, "What do you

Interview Questions for a School Library Position

Elementary School

- Elaborate on the five roles of a school librarian as defined by the *Standards for 21st Century Learners*.
- Define *information literacy*. What does the term mean to you? How does it pertain to elementary school children?
- Technology has a major impact on instruction. What are your prior experiences with technology as it relates to library media administration, circulation, record keeping, instruction, research, and social media?
- Students exhibit a wide range of abilities. How would you differentiate instruction to meet the needs of diverse student populations?
- Describe the steps you would take to build a quality collection.
- Our elementary school library media curriculum is delivered via a fixed schedule of weekly classes. Discuss the benefits and drawbacks of this instructional delivery model and the strategies you might use to optimize student learning within this framework.
- Describe the kinds of professional development that a media specialist could offer to an elementary school staff.

Secondary School

- The school library media program provides physical and intellectual access to information. What is the difference between the two, and how can each type of access be optimized?
- How do social media and Web 2.0 applications impact a high school media program? What steps will you take to ensure that students of this high school develop the technology skills necessary for success in the 21st century?
- Describe the process you will use to ensure that school library media outcomes are integrated into classroom instruction across all content areas.
- Elaborate on the issues surrounding copyright in a school library media center.
- How can you use this position to improve the ability of your students to meet or exceed the standards set by the AASL for 21st-century learners?
- Describe the instructional role of the media specialist at the secondary level. How does this differ from the role at elementary school?
- How will you build support for the media program with all interest groups, including faculty, staff, media colleagues, students, and parents?
- Discuss the ways in which your role as a school library media specialist can be utilized to provide professional development for the entire staff.

Created by Tish Stafford
Program Facilitator for Media
Cecil County Public Schools, Maryland

think a good school library program should be?" or "What does a twenty-first-century library program look like?" can have you stumbling. Know how you would answer these and similar ones.

Harder questions usually focus on challenging circumstances and ask how you would handle them. You might be asked to explain what you would do if a student were acting up or was on an inappropriate website. If the school has active, involved parents, the question might revolve around one of them coming to you upset about a book or how you treated their child. Anticipating these possibilities and rehearsing your answers will keep you from panicking and allow you to present yourself as a calm professional in charge of his or her environment.

Review the sample questions used in actual interviews and consider what your answers might be.

More Actual Interview Questions

1. How do you differentiate your position from that of the technology specialist in regards to collaborating with teachers, and how would you ensure collaboration with the technology specialist?
2. What is your vision for the library?
3. How will you communicate the happenings in the library to staff, parents, students, and administrators?
4. What would you do if a book was challenged?
5. Name 3 books from the mystery, adventure, and realistic fiction genres.
6. How would you go about weeding the collection and what professional resources would you use?
7. How would you collaborate and reach out to teachers in each subject area?
8. What would you do if a colleague continually brought students to your scheduled class time late?
9. What blogs and/or websites do you use to stay current?
10. In a time of tightening budgets, what can you do to get funds for the library?
11. What will you do to advocate and promote reading school-wide?
12. How will you engage reluctant readers and provide access for students with special needs?

As reported on the AASL Forum Electronic Discussion List

Prepare several questions of your own. You will inevitably be asked if you have any. These should reflect your research on the district and the library program. For example, you might ask how the librarian is helping to promote one of the school goals or what the principal thinks is best about the library program and what further directions he or she would like to see. You need not memorize these, but carry them with you in a folio, preferably one that looks very businesslike.

Anticipating Your Interview

1. What are you looking for in an interview outfit?
2. What two easy questions are you anticipating?
3. What two hard ones?
4. Whom do you know who can play the role of interviewer to help you practice? Encourage that person to come with questions as well.
5. Based on the district you chose for your research, what one or two questions might you ask in an interview?

IN-PERSON INTERVIEWS

The day has arrived for your interview. You are nervous but prepared and arrive early. While waiting to speak with the administrator, go over any calming techniques you have. Focusing on breathing is a good basic one. Arrange yourself, your coat if you have one, purse (if you are female), and your briefcase so that you can stand up smoothly without fumbling to move things around.

Make sure your cell phone is off. Probably because people are so accustomed to having it on, they forget this detail, and then must awkwardly apologize when a call comes in. Under no circumstance should you answer your phone or text during the interview. Unbelievably, interviewers have reported that this has occurred.

The principal may come out to greet you or the secretary may bring you directly to where the interview will be held. Once inside the room, settle yourself once again. If there are multiple people present do what you can to arrange your chair so that you can see everyone. When answering a question, speak directly to the person who posed it but briefly look at the others during the course of your answer.

Take out a copy of your resume. Have additional ones available on the off chance that those other than the main interviewer do not have it. That preparedness will not go unremarked. Also, bring copies of a lesson or presentation you have done. These can be from your course work, or, preferably from your field experience. Select one that demonstrates true twenty-first-century learning, including students connecting with multi-type formats or reaching beyond the library walls, collaborating with others, and creating new knowledge.

At some point in the interview, you should be able to find an opportunity to hand this to any and all present. Give a brief overview of the lesson, with grade level, classroom, and curricular connection if any, and the results of your formative and summative assessments. Highlight how it is twenty-first century. If you are hired, you are already creating the foundation for promoting the library program.

Before answering questions, take a small quiet breath. Allow yourself a moment for reflection. You want to focus on the key point being raised. If you need clarification, ask. Your response should be as brief as possible but should fully cover the issue. Do not go into any side journeys.

Throughout the interview be positive about your previous experiences. If you have left or are hoping to leave another library position, do not speak negatively about the district or its administrators and teachers. Put everything in as positive a cast as possible. For example, you might say, "My current district is working hard to deal with severe budget constraints that have limited the direction it is able to take with technology. I want to continue to advance my abilities in this area, and, from my research, I know that this district is still committed to incorporating new technologies that further student success."

If you have not learned before, ask the reason for replacing the current librarian. Time permitting, your interviewer may give you a tour of some of the building—at least the library. When this is not offered, ask if you can see it. Either the secretary will take you or the librarian may come to the office to escort you there. In the time you have together, you can ask additional questions about the program.

Your leave-taking should be as smooth and professional as your greeting. Thank everyone by name. Indicate it was a pleasure to meet them and have the opportunity to discuss your possible future in the district. Close with, "I hope to hear from you further. Do you have any idea by when you plan to make a decision?" The answer may be very vague, but occasionally, you are given a specific date.

The lead (or sole) interviewer will usually stand to indicate the interview is at an end. Shake hands. Do not under any circumstance hug the person—even if you were offered the job on the spot. Believe it or not, hugging and kissing have been known to occur.

If you have a coat, put it on after you have left the office. Thank the secretary and get her name. You may call her as a follow-up in a week or two, and that added touch of using the name is subtly positive and, if you do get the job, will start your relationship off in a good way.

> **You're On!**
> 1. What example of your expertise as a school librarian will you bring to the interview?
> 2. What are the key points you will make to demonstrate that it is a twenty-first-century lesson?
> 3. What reason will you give for leaving your previous employment?

TELEPHONE INTERVIEWS

While a rarity in education, interviews are sometimes conducted by telephone, particularly if you live some distance away. Although you will be given the date and time for this, the call initiator might not be you. In either case, being prepared and on time is imperative, including the obvious but sometimes overlooked going to the bathroom before the call starts.

Inquire as to whether you can send additional information via e-mail in advance of the call and to whom it should go. If at all possible, you want them to have that sample of your work in hand just as they would have it for an in-person interview. The best person to direct this to would be the secretary, who is most likely to keep track of things. Even so, send a follow-up e-mail or call the day before to be sure that they have the lesson you sent.

If you are the one to make the call, be sure that you have the correct number. Dial in at least five (and not more than eight) minutes before the scheduled time. You will probably be speaking to the secretary. State your name and reason for the call. Depending on circumstances, you might be connected immediately or asked to hold for a few minutes. The exigencies of a principal's job may mean you will be told that something has come up and it will be necessary to reschedule. Accept this as an unfortunate fact of life. As long as you are being rescheduled, you are still in the running for the position.

In the case you are to be called, again be ready at least five minutes ahead of time. If after fifteen minutes your phone has not rung, call the school. Inquire whether there has been a change of plans or if by some chance, you had given them an incorrect telephone number. The call may need rescheduling, so have your calendar ready.

In either situation, find a quiet location where you will not be distracted by anyone. Close the door if possible. Let everyone who might interrupt know that you are not to be disturbed until the interview is completed. Have all your necessary papers handy—your resume and the lesson you sent.

The challenge of a telephone interview is the inability to see people or observe their body language. Even if you are fortunate enough to be able to Skype, the picture may not be clear enough for the subtleties you pick up when you are present. You must rely on voice alone, so listen hard.

Listening is always important in any interview and more so when you are doing it by phone. Do not let your brain race with what you are going to say next. Rather, focus on what you are being asked and the comments made after you respond. You have time to start thinking once the interviewer has completed the question. If you are unclear, do not attempt an answer. Ask for clarification. If necessary, you can say, "Do you mean what *I* believe is the future direction of school libraries, or what the leaders in the field are saying?"

Although you are careful not to speak rapidly (if that is your style) when you are being interviewed in person, speaking distinctly is even more important on the phone. Prepare for this by having a friend "interview" you on the telephone. How did you sound? Did you smile when you spoke? It can be heard in your voice.

Since you cannot be seen, have notes handy to jog your memory about what to say and ask. List any key points you want to make. Have all your questions handy. You may intersperse them when the topic comes up, but there will inevitably be some that will wait until you are asked if you have any.

Of course, you never ask about salary. It would be inappropriate even if the administrator is the one who sets it. You find out about it only when you are offered a job.

Talking Your Walk

1. Where is your best distraction-free location?
2. Practice listening to what someone says before jumping in with your response. Is this natural for you?
3. What will you want to highlight in a phone interview?

SELECTING REFERENCES

In the past, human resource departments rarely checked references. The increasing concern over student safety and the tightening job market has drastically changed that practice. You can now expect that all your references will be contacted.

Typically, you indicate on your resume that "References will be furnished on request." Even if one or more of your references has provided you with a letter, the interviewer might prefer to follow up with a call so be prepared to have complete contact information for everyone you are listing as a reference.

Under the circumstances, you want to choose your references carefully. Ask each of them if they would have any reservations in wholeheartedly supporting your candidacy for a school library position or in describing their experiences with you. Follow up with a discussion to learn what they would identify as your strengths. Do they see any weaknesses?

This mini-interview will let you know whether or not to use this person as reference. You cannot afford a lukewarm endorsement. You should have three to four people on your list, but you are better off having one or two fewer than risk one of them giving you a less than glowing assessment of your capabilities.

Draw from a broad cross-section of people for your references. If you are fresh out of grad school, get *one of* your professors. For the remainder consider what you said about yourself in your resume. What skills in your previous career are you suggesting will help make you a better school librarian? Is there someone you worked with who could speak to that?

For most positions, recommendations from the clergy do not carry much weight. However, if you have worked with children in a youth group, secular or religious, see if your supervisor is willing to discuss how well you interacted with young people. You might even consider having a parent be a reference, particularly if you were instrumental in helping their child in a significant way.

As soon as you have your interview scheduled or immediately thereafter, contact your references. Alert them to the possibility that the district will be in touch with them. Review any key points you want them to make. If they have previously given you a letter, offer to send a copy back to them so they have it on hand. In essence, you want to ensure that all your references stay on message.

Ready with References
1. What four people would you want to use as references?
2. How do they reflect the range of your background experience?
3. What two to three abilities of yours would you like them to highlight?

POST-INTERVIEW ACTIVITIES

No matter how well your interview went, do not sit around waiting for a call informing you that you are being offered the job. You have no idea whether others did better or someone has an inside track. Keep up with your job search.

As discussed in *New on the Job*, a well-crafted thank-you note is vital.[1] Most interviewees send one, but you want yours to leave an impression. Refer to something said during the interview—preferably by the administrator.

Expect to wait. If you were given a date by which a decision was to be made (or asked for it), and it is past that time, you can call the secretary to find out if the position was filled. Schools are notorious for not getting back to candidates who are not offered a job. However, the fact you have not heard does not mean you were not selected. Administrators, unless hard-pressed, often take much longer than anticipated to complete the interview process and determine which applicant will be hired.

Eventually, you will find out. You may have a second interview if there are several candidates under consideration. If you do get the position, do not say yes right away. You need to make certain this is the right job for you, as will be discussed in the next chapter.

It is disheartening to be turned down, but the odds are that will happen with several of your interviews. Recognize that reaching the interview stage means that your application was strong enough for the administrator to consider you a viable candidate. What you want to do is learn from the experience so that you will do better next time.

While it does not always work, you can call and ask to briefly speak with the administrator who interviewed you. If you get through start by thanking that person for having given you the opportunity to be interviewed and say you will not be taking up much time, but you want to improve your chances when you apply elsewhere. Is there anything he or she can tell you that you might have handled better? Was there a specific lack that you could overcome?

Whether the follow-up call works or not, reflect on what occurred during the interview. Make a column for the positives and one for the negatives. Consider everything from your dress to your responses. Were there any clues that you did not impress the administrator? Can you strengthen the areas in which you did well? What can you do about your weaknesses? Would additional pre-interview practice help? With your analysis as a guide, you will do much better next time.

Using the Wait Time

1. What do you think are some nonverbal signs that your interview is going well?
2. What are some signs that it is going poorly?
3. What would you say to a secretary when calling to find out if the position has been filled?

KEY IDEAS

- Review your research on the district before an interview.
- Dress for success at your interview.
- Prepare, prepare, prepare—from knowing where the parking is to practicing potential questions.
- Be positive about any place you previously worked.
- Bring examples of your work—with copies you can leave.
- Find a distraction-free location for a phone interview.
- Cultivate listening skills and speaking clearly when on the telephone.
- Select your references with care and be sure they can all endorse you without reservations.
- Continue your job search while waiting for the result of an interview.
- Do not accept a job offer immediately. You need to make sure it is the right one for you.

NOTE

1. Ruth Toor and Hilda K. Weisburg, *New on the Job: A School Library Media Specialist's Guide to Success* (Chicago: American Library Association, 2007).

3
SELECTING THE *RIGHT* JOB

You worked hard on your resume, cover letter, interviewing skills, and thank-you note follow-up. Now you are either dealing with one or more job offers or are getting discouraged and wonder what to do next. In the first scenario, you have been offered a position—or more than one. This is what you have been aiming for since you enrolled in library school. It is time to seize the offer and get started on your career. Not so fast! Signing a contract is a commitment, and you want to move cautiously to be as sure as you can that this is the right position for you, and—if it is not—what you can do about it.

In the second situation, you need not despair. There are alternatives, and these can help jump-start your career even if you think you are floundering. Consider several options such as part-time, substituting, and working nonpublic schools and target those that best fit your circumstances.

UNDERSTANDING AND EVALUATING JOB OFFERS

Not all job offers are equal. You want to be sure you understand what the district and school expect of you. Think back to your interview. Reflect on what was said and not said and try to determine whether they are looking to preserve the status quo or want the school librarian to take a proactive role in leading the district forward.

For example, when you asked what they liked best about the library program, what were their key points? Did they mention integrating technology? What was said about collaborating (or cooperating) with teachers? Were there any comments about the library environment? Was anyone astute enough to mention the role of knowledge building or creating content? If not, and you brought it up, what was the reaction? Were they confused? Or did you get the sense that they were eager to learn more and enthusiastic about the possibilities?

What did they not like about the program? If they could not think of anything, does it mean they have no real clue as to what is going on in the library? Or do they like things as they are and want you to continue in the same direction? Depending on how dynamic the program is and your appraisal of the school librarian, would that be good or bad?

Have you met the person who would be your supervisor? How supportive do you think he or she is of the library? It is more than someone saying, "The library is the heart of our school." Sometimes all that means is that they find it a great place for social functions. You should have followed up such a statement by asking, "How does it function as the heart?"

Now is the time to get clear as to what your responsibilities would be and be sure you know what staffing and support you have if you have not learned this previously. Clerical positions are increasingly rare in middle and high school libraries and have always been so at the elementary level. Are duty teachers assigned to help out? Are there volunteer students or parents? With a fixed schedule, you would have an assigned lunch period and a "duty-free" period. You may have bus duty, which will mean you cannot keep the library open after school. What does that fixed schedule look like? How many periods a day do you see students? How long are the periods? Do you see every class at least once a week? Is any clerical time built into the schedule?

If you have a flex schedule, are you permitted to choose which period to have lunch and when to take your duty-free time? If in a middle or high school, do you have an assigned duty time such as being a hall monitor? That will take you out of the library, and if you are the only librarian, it will have to be closed.

Yes Is Not the Only Answer

1. What are the two *most* important elements you want to have in your new job situation (e.g., strong support for new technology, see students at least once a week)?
2. What red flag would cause you to turn down a job offer?
3. What follow-up question might you ask if you are told there are no volunteers or duty teachers to assist with clerical tasks?

MULTIPLE JOB OFFERS

Receiving multiple job offers was once fairly common. Even today, you might be faced with this situation, and you should be prepared to make a rational assessment that will best fit your career path. This is a big decision and you need to weigh *all* the elements. Let the districts know you are considering your options. Ask to know when they must have a final answer from you and get the contact information for the librarian or whomever can answer your critical questions.

Begin with your first priority—the students. If these are elementary library positions, all will probably have a fixed schedule, but that does not mean your day will look the same. How often do you see classes? For how long? Does one or more of the schools have clerical help and/or volunteers? The answers to these questions will let you know how effective you can be in providing opportunities for twenty-first-century learning. If you are evaluating offers for high school jobs, you need to know the size of the school population and whether there is another librarian and any clerical staff. You also should inquire as to the extent of teacher use of the library and whether faculty members regularly collaborate with the librarian. You could develop this relationship, but it is much easier if one is already in place.

Comparing technology differences is extremely important. How many computers are in the library? How old are they? Is there an interactive whiteboard? Cameras? Data projectors? How supportive is the technology department? What automation system is in use? (Is there one? There are still school libraries that have card catalogs.) How many online databases are available?

Budgets are key indicators as to how strongly the administration supports the library program. Get comparative statistics if at all possible. In the past few years, every department has experienced cuts, but the library should not be disproportionately targeted. Figure out what is spent per pupil. The amount allocated to the library might be affected in other ways. For example, one place might require the library budget to include ink cartridges and paper for printers while others provide them through the school supplies. Check to see if any funding comes from sources that are not obvious. The parent organization might regularly give profits from a book fair to the library. Alumni or class gifts are fairly common in some places and virtually nonexistent in others.

The school's culture is another aspect to assess. One that is collegial and student-centered will be more open to a dynamic library program. Teachers who are jaded and locked into the status quo for whatever reason will make your job more difficult. Just walking into a building can give you a good sense of this. Creative bulletin boards and murals in the hallways send one message. A completely different one is sent by displays that show heavy reliance on commercial products and pedestrian examples of student work.

Consider the environment of the libraries in question. Are they equally welcoming? How much work would it take to make a less inviting place become more appealing to students and others? Would the administration be supportive of a change? Are they willing to invest money in making alterations or would you need to find your own sources of funding?

Finally, think about your reaction to the people who interviewed you. Would you like working with them? Your instincts are usually very good. Trust them.

Once you have made your choice, inform the other districts that you will not be accepting their offer. Be sure to let them know how much you appreciated their time and that you gave serious consideration to taking the position. Explain the reasons why you decided to go elsewhere. It is helpful for administrators to realize that their openness to new technologies or how tightly they schedule librarians can affect the quality of the candidates who will be willing to work under those conditions. Above all be extremely courteous. You never know when you might be applying to this district in the future, or come across the administrator in a new setting.

Decisions, Decisions, Decisions

1. In addition to the factors discussed what other elements might enter into your decision to choose one position over another?
2. With whom would you want to schedule a conversation to get answers to your questions?
3. How would you open and close a letter turning down a job?

NEGOTIATING SALARY AND DETERMINING YOUR MONTHLY PAY

Once you have accepted the offered position, you will meet with someone from the human resources department to complete a myriad of paperwork (including getting fingerprinted) and to determine what your salary will be. If your previous experience has been solely from the corporate world, be prepared to be shocked. You have very little maneuvering room here.

Teachers are paid on a salary scale based on years of experience and level of degree. The lowest level is a fresh-out-of-college person with a bachelor's degree. If you have a master's, the starting salary is higher. Some places will increase pay for each ten credits earned toward a higher degree, encouraging faculty members to keep working toward improving their professional expertise.

Each year of experience is another step on the guide. The monetary increase is not uniform, and typically there is a bigger jump from the third to fourth year when a new hire would attain tenure. Once placed on the guide, you are locked in. The teacher bargaining unit will work to achieve increases for each contract, and you will receive whatever amount is set for the step on which you are for that school year.

With that in mind, you need to go into the meeting with human resources with an eye to being placed as high as possible on the guide. Be prepared to learn that some districts refuse to give credit for any previous experience and start everyone at the first step, allowing only for whatever degree you hold. While this is rare, obviously the idea is to start you as low as possible while you want to achieve the opposite.

If you have experience in schools, most districts will count some or all of your years of experience. What becomes more challenging is to get credit for what you have done if you are new to education. Review your resume for any jobs that can—with some stretch—be considered educational.

For example, if you have been a corporate trainer, you could argue that should count. A bigger reach might be experience as a camp counselor or scout leader. These jobs, paid or volunteer, show that you have knowledge and background in education or working with students.

You are not likely to get full credit for these non-school positions, but if you can make a strong enough case, you might be allowed one year for every two you spent. While this does not sound like much, remember you have no room, other than pursuing an advanced degree, to earn anything more than what is on the guide for wherever you are placed. Each year, in lockstep you will move up one step.

One other aspect of teacher salary may be new to you if you have not previously been a teacher. Your salary is based on a ten-month school year, which means you do not get paid during summer vacation. Some places offer the option of being paid over twelve months. Others offer a way to deduct 10 percent of your monthly salary, depositing it into a local bank or credit union which you can then draw from to cover your summer expenses. Although both of these effectively reduce your take-home pay, most teachers find it a helpful way to manage the two-month break. Human resources will explain your options during your salary meeting.

You may also have additional choices to make. As a public employee you are entitled to invest in a 403 (b) plan, similar to the 401(k) of the corporate world; it is a tax-deferred annuity that reduces your taxable income and provides regular savings. Unlike a 401(k), the employer makes no contribution to this. Some districts provide the ability to put money in a company such as AFLAC for health-related expenses not included in whatever health plan is offered. You might also have the option of selecting from an insurance package that pays you when you have exceeded your sick days or are hospitalized. These choices you make depending on your needs will affect your take-home pay.

> **Show Me the Money**
> 1. What work experiences have you had that might help to boost your starting salary?
> 2. What community service work have you done for several years that could be described as educational experience?
> 3. Which of the possible options would you consider? Which would you reject?

PART-TIME EMPLOYMENT

Sometimes, to your surprise, you learn at the end of the interview that the position being offered is a part-time one. Should you take it? While this omission of information should give you pause about accepting the job, the fact that it is not full-time is not necessarily a negative.

Of course you want a full-time position, but in this job market you may not have that option. Indeed, you might knowingly apply as a part-time librarian. As with any offer, you will need to look at it carefully.

On the positive side, as a part-timer you get to know the students, teachers, and administrators and can practice those relationship skills. You have a bit more leeway for making mistakes, particularly at the beginning, since it is understandable for you not to know everyone or be aware of all procedures. As you settle in, you can quietly determine the culture of the school and district, identify the "star" teachers, and learn the direction administrators want to take the school and district.

What you are doing is deciding if you want to continue in the position and, if possible, work toward it becoming full-time. Meanwhile, you can continue to search for another job. Leaving in the middle of the year because you have found a better situation is not a detriment to your future career plans if you are part-time.

When you apply elsewhere, you are a stronger candidate because you are employed. At an interview, you will be more relaxed and confident. You are not desperate for a job, so you are the one interviewing the school rather than the other way around. Even if you like your part-time situation, continue to look for other situations. The real-life interview experience is invaluable and you might find a position you like much better than your current one.

You can let your administrators know you are job-hunting, letting them know that you are looking for full-time employment. Ask your supervisor for a reference. You will need to show that you are doing well where you are. As a side benefit, if administrators believe you are a doing a great job but might lose you to another district, they may work on making your position full-time.

Before you rush into accepting a part-time situation, consider the downside and ask a lot of questions. What exactly does part-time mean? Is it a three-day or a one-day job? Are you in a single school or dividing what is already limited time between one or more schools? If you are divided between buildings, do you need to travel between them in the course of the day? Will you be compensated for mileage?

Do you have any benefits? You are not likely to get the health plan offered to full-timers, but do you get any sick leave or personal days? Do you get a lunch break or a duty-free period?

Find out who your supervisor is. If you are in more than one school, you will have to adjust to the leadership style of each principal. This can cause conflicts because of different styles. You also might find yourself in a tug-of-war between administrators who try to get you to stay in their building longer. Also, you need to know which faculty meetings you attend and to which schools you report for parent conferences. You may not be able to discover all this at the outset. If you are caught in the middle, simply ask the administrators in question to work out the best division of your time and let them know you will comply with their decision.

Question administrators carefully as to your job responsibilities. You may discover that you are expected to handle a computer lab or teach a class in addition to your regular library assignment. Sometimes these additional duties are the reason the position is open. The previous librarian may have decided to leave rather than accept what are probably new conditions resulting from budget cuts.

Do you accept an offer even though there are many red flags? That depends on your situation. If you really need a job, you probably will take it on, but have some plan for dealing with the downside. At least you are not walking in unaware of the expectations. You can maintain a positive spin on the situation by focusing on what you are getting out of it. Consider it a learning experience. Meanwhile keep all options open and continue to job hunt.

Part Way In

1. What would be the thing you most want to learn if you accepted a part-time position?
2. What reason would you have for taking it if you knew it would never be full-time?
3. List two to three concerns that would keep you from taking a part-time situation.

SHORT-TERM POSITIONS

A variation on the part-time position is to accept one for a limited duration, covering a pregnancy or extended sick leave. Such openings may range from several months to a year and are usually an excellent option when jobs are scarce. Frequently, you can contact the librarian who is on leave for information and advice.

Although you can introduce new small-scale programs demonstrating your areas of strength, do not change any existing procedures. The person you are replacing will probably be returning and will take it amiss if you have disrupted his or her operation methods. While you will have your own style for interacting with students and teachers, you should keep such things as scheduling classes, sign-in procedures, and handling of overdues the way they have been done in the past.

As with a part-time job, focus on seeing what you can learn in a real-life situation. Observe how teachers handle their classes and challenging students. Listen to lunchroom conversations to find out attitudes toward administrators. Identify which teachers are complainers and which ones are forward-looking and interested in trying new approaches to engage their students. When you have that permanent position, you will be able to integrate this information more rapidly and know who to seek out when you want to plan collaborative lessons.

See what works and what does not in dealing with students. What you learned in graduate school or even in the classroom if you have been a teacher, does not always translate into conditions in a school library. The time you spend in this temporary position should be your own learning laboratory.

Going on interviews when you have contracted for a short-term position should be handled more carefully than in a part-time situation. If it is for one semester, you can begin looking after the first month with the understanding that you are seeking a job after this one is over. You should wait several months before applying elsewhere when you are expected to cover the leave for a year.

Keep a portfolio of your lessons and programs. When you do go on an interview, you will be able to show what you accomplished in a limited time. Again, ask your administrator or supervisor for a recommendation—always making sure that it will be a strong one.

If at all possible, maintain contact with the person you are temporarily replacing. Sometimes these short-term positions become permanent. For example, a maternity leave may be extended into a child-rearing leave. After the allowed period is over, the new parent occasionally decides to become a stay-at-home mom. Technically, the district would then post the opening. But as the person who has been filling the slot, as long as you have been doing a good job, you will have the inside track.

> **In the Short Run**
> 1. In what ways do you think a short-term position is better than part-time?
> 2. In what ways is part-time better?
> 3. What relationship(s) would you want to focus on developing while in a short-term job?

SUBSTITUTING

One option that is always present, particularly if the job hunt is taking a long time, is to sign up to be a substitute in one or more districts. The primary drawback is that you will spend most of your time in the classroom rather than the library, but you can make it a positive. Consider that you are in the perfect position to observe all aspects of the school which you can use to your advantage later.

Being in the classroom gives you insights into different approaches teachers take with their curriculum, how they design their lessons, and establish routines. Even if you have been a teacher, this gives you an opportunity to see how others do things. Without this knowledge you would only know what you did. As a librarian, you deal with all teachers and must be able to adapt to their methods and organizational procedures.

In addition to seeing the lesson plans, reading any notes a teacher has left for you can also be instructive. Some may caution you about students or suggest a course of action if a disruption should occur. You can often tell what the teacher's attitude is to his or her class by how these comments are written. At the elementary level, students will also tell you how various situations are handled.

While you should never discuss any practices you consider as negative, you can learn from poor teachers almost as much as from good ones. Compare how students respond in classes where they feel respected by their teacher with ones where the teacher is ineffective or something of a bully. Here is where you learn what works and what does not.

Learning to handle discipline as a substitute is another invaluable lesson. Most students, elementary through high school, tend to act up somewhat when their regular teacher is not in the classroom. While you can threaten to report any bad conduct to their teacher, you will do far better to develop strategies to hold their interest and be involved with what you are teaching.

In some ways, plunging into the classroom this way is a trial by fire. If at all possible, avoid asking administrators for help. You want to show your competence. A friendly faculty member can often suggest effective methods and might know some of your more challenging students. During lunch periods, seek out the collective wisdom of teachers. People enjoy being thought of as experts and like to give advice and help. Trust that you will get better with experience.

Maintaining order in the library environment is far more challenging than in a classroom. Elementary students dropped off by their teacher into the open layout of your facility may behave as though they are in the playground, calling out to one another, running, and having difficulty listening to your directions. At the upper levels you get "drop-in" students who are allegedly there to do research but often see their pass as a "get-out-of-jail-free" card from class or a time to socialize with friends who may be there. (Sometimes, they plan this ahead of time.) Your experience in dealing with assorted discipline issues as a substitute will give you confidence in managing students whatever their age.

To increase your chances of being in the library, let whoever is in charge of calling substitutes know that you prefer a library assignment whenever it is possible. Suggest that you can work in the library if you do not have a full schedule on a given day. The librarian will appreciate it, and you get an opportunity to see a program in operation.

Substituting in more than one school—and in several districts—can be eye-opening. Even schools with relatively similar socioeconomic populations can operate in radically different ways. When you can compare one with another, it becomes obvious what the school culture is in each. You can see how administrative styles affect the morale, motivation, and climate of a building.

After you have been in a few schools several times, you will know which ones are places where you would like to work. Let the principal know how much you like the school and that if a position becomes available you would like to be considered for it. As with some "temp" jobs in the business sector, being a substitute allows administrators an opportunity to see how you work. Many districts give preference to those who have been successful substitutes.

No Substitute for Real-Life Experience

1. For which schools in your area would you want to apply as a substitute?
2. How would you ask for advice on handling classroom discipline?
3. What do you think is the most congenial culture for you? Hierarchical? Collegial?

PRIVATE, PAROCHIAL, AND CHARTER SCHOOLS

Although many private, parochial, and charter schools do not have librarians (or libraries), a number of them do, and working in one is an excellent alternative if you are having difficulty finding a job. After one or two years, you will have honed your skills and have real experience to put on your resume. Keep a record not only of your successful lessons, but also of stories that show how your program touched students' lives and made a difference. Stories tend to have a strong impact and being able to drop them into an interview will increase your chances of being hired when you are ready to look for a position in a public school.

While there are differences among these three types of schools, there are also commonalities. Invariably there is strong parental interest and involvement with the school. Private and parochial schools can easily ask students to leave if they do not follow the rules or meet criteria that have been set. Charter schools, since they receive taxpayer dollars, must accept those who fall within the guidelines of the charter but can return students to public school if they (or their parents) are not complying with the rules.

In general, this means you have a more motivated group of students. When you are in your first year in a school, being able to focus on your teaching rather than discipline speeds your own learning process. You still need to have classroom management skills, but there will be fewer challenging situations and you can call on administrative support more freely.

Although private and parochial schools often have a shorter school day and somewhat longer vacations, the opposite is true for charter schools. Since each of them has a specific agenda or mission, the demands placed on staff may be surprising. Some have school days that go as late as 5 p.m. Others require parental visits. You need to know what the requirements are before signing a contract.

Parent involvement is important for student success, but it can also be a negative for the faculty. Mothers and fathers are more likely to scrutinize their children's work and contest a low grade. They often have more authority than in a public school and use it when they are concerned. (Helicopter parents who hover over every assignment can be a problem in public schools as well, particularly in the more affluent districts.)

On the downside, salary and benefits are two big drawbacks to teaching in these school situations. Private and parochial school pay scales do not come close to that of public schools. Charter schools may pay the same, but the hours and length of the school year tend to be longer. You might also find a difference in the number of sick and personal days allowed. While public employees are paying more these days for health benefits, they still do get them. The availability of such benefits in private and parochial schools varies and pension plans are rare.

These disadvantages are not really an issue if you plan on seeking a public school position. On the whole, the positives outweigh any of the shortcomings if you want to increase your skills and build your resume while searching for a job. Check the schools in your area and see what openings they have.

Private Alternative

1. Research differences among private, public, and charter schools in your area. Which, if any, might be a good fit for you if they have librarians?
2. How would you handle overly involved parents?
3. How do you feel about working a longer day or year?
4. What are your minimum requirements for health benefits?

KEY IDEAS

- Reflect back on what was said and not said in the interview to help decide among multiple job offers.
- Consider potential administrators' attitudes toward the library in making your decision.
- Assesses the school's culture and the library environment as factors in determining which offer(s) to accept.
- Existing technology and budget history are clues to how much the administration supports the library program.
- Identify any experiences that can be considered education-related when negotiating your starting salary.
- Part-time employment can improve your resume while you continue to job hunt.
- Short-term positions are similar to part-time but allow you to feel more a part of the school community.
- Substituting gives you more classroom than library time but can make you a more attractive candidate for future employment in the school.
- All interim positions (part-time, short-term, or substituting) can help you polish your skills, get a deeper understanding of how schools work, and improve your chances for a full-time job.
- Working in non-public schools usually means some sacrifices in the area of pay, benefits, and, sometimes, length of school day and year, but gives you extensive experience.

4
MASTERING THE LEARNING CURVE

Once you have landed a job, reality sets in. No matter how hard you worked in library school, you have much to learn to be successful in your job. As a school librarian you have many roles: teacher, information specialist, instructional partner, and program administrator.[1] In order to carry out these roles, from day one you need to set a course to becoming a leader and making the library program an essential component of every class, recognized by teachers, students, administrators, and even the community at large—always demonstrating you are a teacher and facilitator for twenty-first-century learning.

To achieve what seems such a large goal as you embark on your career requires focus. You must take personal responsibility for your own growth and development. From your very first day, you must become an astute observer. The education world has been under attack for some time, driven by demands from national and state governments as well as parents. Different approaches to pedagogy surface regularly as do more government requirements. You have studied many of these movements in your classes; now you will discover how they impact your work life and that of your students and colleagues. You need to keep abreast of any new ones—and help faculty (and sometimes administrators) know what is on the horizon.

Technology as it affects school libraries and education is changing ever more rapidly. What you learned in library school will not keep you current with what you need to know. Your awareness of these trends and how to integrate them into the curriculum make you vital to teachers and students. But finding out about these new resources and gaining proficiency in using them is *your* responsibility. In essence, you need to hit the ground running—and never stop.

LISTEN AND OBSERVE TO LEARN

To be successful, your "running" needs purpose and direction or else you are likely to bang into walls. If you are fortunate, there is a mission statement for your library that will guide your priorities, otherwise you will need to create it. You can start with the one in *Empowering Learners*.[2] Once you have a better sense of what you want to accomplish, tweak or rewrite this statement or the one you inherited. The statement you ultimately craft should send a succinct, jargon-free message clearly defining what makes your program unique and vital.

In the early stages, develop a balance between being a presence in the building and discovering the powerful teachers, the go-to secretaries, and the truly supportive administrators. While you are still honing your mission statement, become an active listener and observer. Learn what is happening in the classrooms and all other areas of the school. Every building has its own undercurrents, positive and negative. There is a history between faculty members, and it is wise to move cautiously until you have a good sense of all the players.

If at all possible, vary when you take lunch so you eat with different teachers—and do take lunch. It is imperative that you meet and get to know as many of the staff (professional and others) and have them know you. Only if you are aware of what teachers are doing in their classes are you able to either present complementary lessons to elementary students or, where there is a flexible schedule, suggest collaborative modifications to units showcasing how the library program can increase student learning.

Active listening is a well-documented approach to having meaningful conversations and creating working relationships. It normally involves repeating back to someone what you believe you heard, paraphrasing it, and then reflecting on the content. Make sure you understand what is being said. What is also necessary for you to become knowledgeable about your school is to be conscious of tone of voice and language choice when others are discussing people and practices. While absorbing this content, your own conversation should be as neutral as possible, with the exception of allowing your passion to show about the goals of the library program. When you identify someone who seeks innovative approaches to making learning more meaningful for students, seek to build a connection.

Active observation is intrinsic to the practice of medicine and is likened to being in the mode of Sherlock Holmes.[3] It is a skill well worth cultivating as you establish your program and place within your school. Obviously, you will be aware of body language, but also see what cliques exist among the faculty. Who sits with whom? Are they open to new people joining them or is it a closed group? How do others regard them? Careful, but not conspicuous, observation gets you quickly up to speed in the dynamics of school. In becoming not just familiar with most of the staff (depending on the size of the school) but also aware of their attitudes and interpersonal relationships, you will choose wisely among those who will be most likely to work with you towards carrying out your mission.

Proceeding this way may sound cold-blooded and calculated, but being careful in the early phases is not about playing politics or strategically planning to have only powerful associates within the staff. What you are working to avoid are missteps that will negatively label you. As you become comfortable in your new position, you will make friends with those who share your interests and like working with you. They need not be the school's "stars," but you will not have been lured into associations with malcontents looking for new allies. You do need to be cordial to everyone. Part of your responsibilities is to have a professional relationship with *everyone* in the building. The library must always be a welcoming place for all.

Eyes and Ears

1. Practice active listening to become skilled at it. What did you hear that you would have missed? What have you learned from it?
2. Eavesdrop on random conversations. Close your eyes and focus on tone of voice. What could you tell about the speaker?
3. Observe a group of people. What messages are sent by their body language?

LEARNING ON THE JOB

Watching good and bad teachers in action will teach you far more than anything you learned in your graduate classes about how to conduct a lesson. Observe teacher interactions with their students. If you have a flexible schedule this is relatively easy. The teacher will be accompanying and remaining with the class. With fixed schedules, you will need to rely on observing what happens at drop-off and pick-up. You can also ask permission from various teachers to sit in on their class during your duty-free time.

Your active listening and watching alerted you to the importance of body language. Is the teacher at ease with the class or working at being in control? How does the teacher deal with student questions? Some give them short shrift, concerned only with getting back to delivering the lesson. Others are better at acknowledging the question and answering it appropriately. Some excellent teachers will encourage students to reason it out themselves and share their thoughts.

In general, observe who is doing most of the talking. Is it the teacher? The girls? The boys? Or is the entire class engaged? Check students' body language. Are they focused on what is going on or are they zoning out? What is the teacher doing to cause these reactions? Are there underlying routines that make the class run smoothly, or are there disruptions whenever a lesson moves from lecture to group work? Is the teacher respectful of students? How can you tell?

If possible, ask to see the lesson plan or talk with the teacher about what the objectives and essential questions were for the class. Assess whether or not these were achieved and why or why not. What lessons are there for you in this observation? If the teacher wants to hear your impressions of what went on, focus on the positives. In all cases, thank the teacher for the opportunity.

In addition to learning from teachers, you can also learn from administrators. Get a sense of how the faculty feels about the principal, vice-principal, and other supervisors. There will always be those who will find fault but determine the overall view, particularly that of the good teachers. Identify the qualities they find admirable and those that they dislike. Usually honesty and trusting the staff rather than caving instantly to parents or others rank high.

Watch how the administrators conduct meetings. Note whether they are focused and to the point or drag out, losing the attention of everyone. Do you get a sense of how whatever is under discussion promotes the administrator's vision and purpose? When something needs to be done, do you feel that you were enrolled in the project or forced into it?

By seeing how good leaders inspire people and poor ones create pockets of antagonism, you can start picking up skills that will help you as you move your career forward. You might have been aware of some of this from a previous career you had, but schools work somewhat differently from the business world and you want to heighten your sensibilities to these differences.

Try to understand the dynamics of teacher interactions with each other and the administration so that when you seek to collaborate or cooperate with them you are sensitive to underlying issues. Eventually, you will run meetings, either when chairing a committee or setting up a project. The meeting may be formal or informal, barely appearing to be one, but you will be the one in charge and your responsibility will be to keep everyone inspired and focused on what is to be accomplished. You build your skills by observing those who do this very well and those who do it poorly.

The Good, the Bad, and the Ugly
1. Think of a teacher you admired and list the qualities that made you feel that way.
2. Think of a teacher you thought was awful and list the qualities that made you feel that way.
3. What must occur for people to leave a meeting feeling enthusiastic and energized?

FINDING A MENTOR

In addition to observing good and bad practices, one of the best things you can do for yourself is to get a mentor. Some state library associations have programs that provide them. Otherwise, reach out and locate one yourself. If you have not yet met the school librarians in your district, find out who they are and call them and introduce yourself. Some places have a monthly meeting for librarians, which is another way to get to know them. Assess how well they seem to be delivering their programs, and then ask one who is doing an outstanding job to be your mentor.

In places where there is a district supervisor for librarians, ask for a suggestion as to which librarian would be a good mentor for you. This not only gets you the help you need, it shows your supervisor your enthusiasm and interest in becoming skilled in your job as soon as possible. The suggested mentor will undoubtedly be flattered to have been recommended by the supervisor and will be eager to show the confidence was well placed.

If you have joined your state's school library association (or section of the larger library association), note the people who post often to the electronic discussion board. Look for the ones with good ideas who are tuned into what is happening on the national and state scene. Send an e-mail to that person and ask if he or she will be your mentor. What you are looking for is someone with whom you feel compatible and who seems to be doing a good job.

Being a school librarian at any grade level is very different from being a classroom teacher. Your administrator expects that you know all aspects of your job, yet for new librarians that is rarely the case. Asking for help suggests you are not expert in your field, which is contrary to the image you are working to build. A mentor is a non-judgmental guide, so you are free to discuss where you are struggling, where your stresses are, and in which situations you feel clueless. You do not have to hold anything back, because your mentor is there for you.

The relationship will give you someone to call when you are confused about procedures or just want suggestions on how to prioritize your workload. If both of you are willing, set up regular calls or even go out for coffee after school once a month. In most situations, you are the only librarian in the building. It is helpful to have a person who understands your daily demands and has the expertise to help.

Although your mentor will be willing to guide you through your initial year (or years) on the job, recognize that you are the one in need and therefore must be as accommodating as possible. For example, ask what your mentor's preferred method of communication is. While most will choose e-mail, some like a phone call or even to Skype. Whatever it is, make sure you use that route as much as possible.

Be mindful of your mentor's time. Do not call or e-mail every day. Your mentor has a busy schedule—particularly if he or she is a leader. The relationship should be supportive, not a burden. For example, develop a lesson and ask for a critique before presenting it, rather than writing one together. You do not want to be so dependent on the mentor that you fail to gain confidence in your own abilities and style. Afterwards, discuss what worked, what did not, and what you might have done differently. In a short time, this post-lesson analysis will be all you will need.

Some mentors will want to set up a regular call or check-in. Others will do it on the fly as necessary. You can and should incorporate time to get to know each other better, but do not extend your communication unless you have checked that you are not infringing on that person's time.

Those who have entered school librarianship from an "alternate" route and do not have education credentials may be required by their state to have a mentor. Frequently this means your mentor is not a librarian—and you might be required to pay him or her a stipend. Where this is the situation, you still need a school librarian mentor because a teacher will not understand the scope of your job.

Merits of Mentors

1. Have you ever had or been a mentor, officially or unofficially? If the experience was successful what made it work? What were some difficulties?
2. Whom do you know in the field who might be willing to mentor you?
3. If you had the choice, what method of communication would you prefer?

GAINING EXPERIENCE AND GROWING ON THE JOB

Although your graduate school courses provided you with much knowledge about librarianship, you are now faced with fitting those academic concepts into the practical day-to-day world of the school—and doing it as seamlessly as possible. While you might want to stay in the library until you get your bearings, remaining within your walls will not get you known. You want to gain experience and become part of the fabric of the school. Speed your learning curve and have faculty and administrators see how your expertise can make a contribution while getting that needed experience by becoming a member of a school or district committee.

Consider your interests, the mission of the library program, and the effectiveness of the various committees in determining on which one you would like to serve. Technology planning is usually a good fit, but other potential possibilities include curriculum writing, literacy, or one charged with developing strategies for improving student scores on high-stakes tests. The latter may not sound interesting, but while *you* know the research has shown that active school library programs, staffed by a certificated librarian, have a significant effect on student achievement on these tests, others might not be aware of this. Serving here will be an excellent opportunity to present that information.[4] Additionally, being on this committee gives you an understanding of the types of questions students in your school are finding difficult. With this knowledge, you can tweak your library program to address the need and then let administrators know how you are contributing to raising test scores.

A curriculum-writing committee gives you immediate access to both current and future plans for a subject or grade level. You learn what the "essential questions" are and can make suggestions for integrating technology and research. Your perspective is different from teachers, and this unique contribution lets them see the value of the library program. At the same time you are generally working with the better teachers and often a supervisor, so you pick up practical techniques for motivating students as they discuss the structure and content of units.

Similarly, literacy committees bring together teachers who are interested in fostering lifelong readers, literacy coaches who know the myriad of developmental skills, and administrators familiar with the high-stakes tests assessing which skills students have or have not mastered. With this group you bring your broad background in children's or young adult literature. Again, you will be demonstrating how library resources connect to learner outcomes they are trying to achieve.

Before volunteering for a committee, keep one caveat in mind. Not all of them are equally effective. Find out who is on the different ones and what has been achieved by each. Being on a nonproductive committee is a waste of your valuable time.

If you have not done so already, join your state's school library association and its electronic discussion list. Make sure you have checked the membership form carefully to be sure you have indicated your desire to be put on the list, as this does not always happen automatically. These electronic discussion lists are a vital source for what is happening in your state regarding schools and school libraries. You will quickly be able to identify the "movers and shakers." Also, if you have a question such as books on a topic to recommend to teachers or any other aspect of your job, post it here. Responses come rapidly and you will have a wealth of advice from which to choose.

> **Learning by Doing**
> 1. Which of the committees mentioned would seem to be a good fit for you?
> 2. What would you be able to contribute?
> 3. What would you possibly learn?

EARNING TENURE

Tenure is always in the back of the mind of new hires. Despite what the general public seems to believe, it is no guarantee of a permanent job, but having it does make you feel more secure. Once you are tenured, you cannot be fired without "due process." Before you reach that milestone, you can be denied a new contract without any reason being given. Some districts are notorious for rarely giving tenure, allowing them to keep salary costs low. If you are employed at one, you will get rumors of it early and should start keeping your eye out for openings somewhere else.

When staff is cut or departments eliminated, tenure will not keep you from being terminated. Up until now, the practice has been last in, first out. In some cases where library positions were slashed, librarians who held teaching certification "bumped" a teacher. The outcry over getting rid of "good teachers" and keeping tired and worn-out ones (often a code for "higher-salaried faculty") is likely to lead to changes.

As a new employee, you will be observed by your supervisor (and in some places by an assistant superintendent) several times each year. Although your job involves much more than teaching, invariably that will be the only evaluation on record of how you are doing. You are unlikely to get a completely glowing assessment of your lesson. Almost every administrator makes a point of noting what was good about it and where you can improve it. Read both what was commended and recommended carefully, and avoid becoming defensive over criticism.

When you have your conference to discuss the observation, focus on the administrator's suggestions for improvement. Use active listening skills, restating what was said to ensure you fully understand what you are being told to do. Ask if he or she would like you to send a brief report on how you have followed the suggestions and what the results were.

The same criticism should not be repeated in your next observation. If it is, you probably have a problem that needs to be addressed immediately. Hopefully, your administrator will feel that you dealt with the issue, although another recommendation will undoubtedly be made. Follow the same procedure as you did the first time. Acknowledge (without toadying) where the original one was helpful and any modifications you made to allow for the differences between teaching in a classroom and the library environment.

Find out when you can expect your end-of-year evaluation, which usually has a place for the administrator to indicate whether you will be offered a contract for the next year. At least a week in advance, send a report to your supervisor detailing what you have done outside of school to improve your program. This is where you would refer to conference attendance (particularly if you took personal days to attend), any committees you might serve on at the state or national level, and courses, webinars, and other professional development initiatives you undertook on your own.

The report will alert the administrator to your commitment to professional growth and give him or her information to be incorporated into your evaluation. This is the only way to document accomplishments other than teaching. Of course, the evaluation will also include a "prescription" for improvement. Unless it is way out of line and sounds as though it is paving the way for ultimately not granting you tenure, react to it the way you did suggestions in the observations.

If you are concerned about an observation or an end-of-year evaluation, take it to one of the union leaders in your building for advice on how to handle it. Being contentious will not improve your chances of getting a contract. In districts that are not unionized, find an experienced teacher you trust and ask for suggestions as to what you should do.

Although many states are now extending the number of years necessary before earning tenure, usually it is three years plus one day. On the first day of your fourth contract year, you will have tenure. As noted earlier, tenure itself is under fire so the requirements for earning it are likely to change. Tying it to test scores is problematic for school librarians unless you know which questions can be connected to your teaching, which is a good idea for you to learn whether or not it counts for tenure. Whatever changes come, be sure you stay current with them so you meet any new requirements.

> **On the Tenure Track**
> 1. What, if anything, surprised you about tenure?
> 2. What do think are the pros and cons about tenure?
> 3. Do you think you would do your job differently with or without it?

KEY IDEAS

- Take responsibility for your own professional growth and development.
- Be an active listener and observer.
- Try to eat at different lunches and vary with whom you eat.
- Learn what practices work and which ones do not by observing good and bad teachers.
- Observe how administrators present themselves and their ideas in large and small groups to determine good and bad practices.
- Get a mentor.
- Become a member of a school or district committee.
- Join your state's school library association and its electronic discussion list.
- Pay attention to what your supervisor commends and recommends in your observation and avoid becoming defensive over criticism.
- In advance of your year-end evaluation, send a report to your supervisor detailing what you have done outside of school to improve your program.

NOTES

1. *Empowering Learners: Guidelines for School Library Media Programs* (Chicago: American Library Association, American Association of School Librarians, 2009), 16–18.
2. Ibid., 7.
3. KSUM–W Volunteer Faculty Preceptor, "Using Active Observation of Students," http://wichita.kumc.edu/preceptor/activeObservation.html.
4. Scholastic Research Foundation, "School Libraries Work!" 2008, www2.scholastic.com/content/collateral_resources/pdf/s/slw3_2008.pdf.

5

GROWING YOUR CAREER

After you have been on the job for about a year, you know the rhythm from school opening to closing. You have watched, learned, and have taken your first steps toward becoming a presence in your building. From here forward, everything you do is directed to growing your program and career.

Your professional development takes on new meaning now that you are further from having professors keep you informed of trends in technology, librarianship, and education. To be successful you consciously become a lifetime learner. Every avenue that increases your knowledge base needs to be explored. While this seems like a huge task—and it is—there is satisfaction in knowing that you are in control of your learning and can direct it as you see fit.

PROFESSIONAL DEVELOPMENT, DISTRICT

During the course of the school year, your district will set aside days for staff development. Rarely will these connect directly to what you do, but you can always find something worthwhile. Overall, these workshops are designed to improve classroom instruction. You may have the option of selecting which ones seem most helpful, or you can be assigned the ones you are expected to attend.

Many teachers have a tendency to make light of these days, regarding them as something of a day off and rejecting the thought that the presenters have anything useful to offer. Do not get sucked into that attitude. You can learn from all of them no matter how far removed a workshop might seem from what you do.

Presentations on differentiated instruction, understanding by design, or essential questions and enduring understandings are easily incorporated into your own teaching. Although the content might be skewed to the classroom, you can adapt it to your program and by doing so truly understand it. A workshop on literacy is extremely informative because most library school courses do not delve into the pedagogy of reading. It is enlightening to discover the many skills and competencies students must master. Knowing this allows you to evaluate your collection with an eye to supporting classroom and reading teachers.

In some rare cases you might have to attend a workshop on a new series the district has purchased led by someone from the publisher. Being present gives you insight into what the teachers will be doing and the resources they will be using. Consider where you can connect the content and objectives to your program. What supportive research projects might improve students' understanding of a unit? When you make these ties, let your supervisor know.

Keep in mind that much communication is nonverbal. You will see many faculty members dressed extremely casually. The subtle message this sends to administrators is that they are not taking the workshops seriously. Wearing your usual school clothes is the best approach, but you can dress down somewhat. You still should appear as a professional.

To make professional development days more relevant to what you do, talk with the other librarians in your district. Identify a topic that is important to all of you, such as deepening your understanding of the *AASL Standards for the 21st-Century Learner*. Prepare a brief description of what you are seeking to learn and why. Submit it to your supervisor with a request to have a session on it. Offer to locate a presenter. Colleagues on your state association's electronic discussion list will be happy to supply names and contact information.

Growing In-House

1. Which do you think will help you more on the job, a workshop on technology, one on literacy, or pedagogy in general? Why?
2. How does dress affect attitude?
3. What challenges do you think you might face in selecting a workshop topic for all the librarians and getting it approved?

PROFESSIONAL DEVELOPMENT ON YOUR OWN

Beyond what the district offers, you need to assume responsibility for more relevant professional development. Funding for outside workshops, and frequently approval for time away from school, are disappearing. Not being compensated is no excuse for not continuing your education. Because of the rapidity of technological changes, being an outstanding school librarian requires continuous updating of your knowledge of new resources and techniques for incorporating them into your program.

Webinars are a relatively inexpensive source of professional development. Your state association's electronic discussion list will alert you to any being offered by your state library. A consortium to which you belong might also inform members of upcoming webinars.

The American Association of School Librarians (AASL) presents webinars that are highly relevant. Some are designed for purchase by a group, but you can search for them at the website www.aasl.org to see what is available. Special ones are sometimes offered for events such as School Library Month in April.

Consider taking advantage of AASL's e-Academy, which offers inexpensive online courses that generally run for about four weeks. For an additional fee, you can earn graduate credits. Search under "e-Academy" on the AASL website (www.ala.org/aasl) to find out what is on the schedule. If you only see old courses, there is an e-mail address to get further information.

Conferences are designed to allow you to select the professional development workshops that best meet your needs. Most states have an annual conference generally lasting two to three days. Your biggest challenge will be choosing which programs to attend because many excellent ones will be given concurrently. Banquets and luncheons feature authors as speakers who typically sign their latest books at the conclusion. The exhibit area is an opportunity to see what new offerings vendors have. Within the conference setting, it is easy to have them give you a demonstration and, if you choose, set up a meeting at your school.

You might have to take a personal day or go on the usually scheduled weekend day. If the district will not reimburse you for your conference expenses, you can take it off your income tax. When you return home, write up a brief summary of the highlights, emphasizing how you will incorporate what you learned to increase student learning.

Check the ALA website at www.ala.org for its Annual and Midwinter conferences. Perhaps one will be scheduled in a city near you. If at all possible try to go even if it is distant. For the Annual Conference, add to your days there to include sightseeing and turn it into a vacation. AASL has a conference on alternate years and that one is fully focused on you and your program. Every presentation is tied to school librarianship. Every exhibitor is there for you.

The free books and posters will enliven your library for months. Although you are likely to bear all the costs, you will return rejuvenated, eager to implement all you have learned—and don't forget to let your administrators know about it. If at all possible, include one of the trips to school sites to see exemplary school librarianship in action.

Do not overlook professional reading. As part of your job you should be reading reviews of books and other media in at least one library journal and preferably more. The articles are equally important for you to read.

If you join (and you should) national organizations such as AASL, ISTE (International Society for Technology in Education) and AECT (Association for Educational Communications and Technology), you will receive their journals as part of your member benefits. Their content offers information on the latest in technology, examples of research into practice, and a host of other relevant information to inspire you, keep you moving forward, and ensure that your program stays at the cutting edge.

Plan to read some professional books over your summer vacation. The national associations previously named publish numerous titles over the year. Education associations such as NEA (National Education Association) and ASCD (Association for Supervision and Curriculum Development) also bring out books that connect to what you do. Since these are targeted more for the classroom, you will have to make the necessary adaptations, but you will also have a wealth of ideas to share with teachers when you return to school. Because ASCD's focus is on administrators, you are likely to be more prepared for in-district professional days as well as show your professionalism by discussing what you learned with your supervisor.

In addition to the national associations, become familiar with publishers that deal with the library market. ABC-CLIO and Neal-Schuman (now part of ALA, which also publishes excellent resources) are two well-known

---

Learning on Your Own

1. Find at least one webinar that you think would be helpful. Check to see if it will be archived if you have a time conflict.
2. Go to your state association's website and find out when it is holding its next conference. If you cannot get all the days off to attend, which one day would you go?
3. Are there any other conferences you can plan to attend?
4. Which professional journals do you read regularly? Occasionally?
5. Identify at least two titles issued by national associations or independent publishers that you think would be helpful.

ones. Go to their websites and see which titles explore topics in which you are currently interested.

Learning can never stop. Not for your students, and not for you. From the moment you leave graduate school, you need to assume responsibility for your professional development so that your students will get the skills and competencies they need for our rapidly changing world. You must become a role model for lifelong learning.

GOING FOR THE MASTER'S DEGREE

Those who only have a "concentration in school library media" or whatever your state accepts as a certificate should now consider going for a master's degree. Since you are working, it should be easier to pay for the courses and your district may pick up the tab for one or two classes per semester. If you still have financial concerns, look to the many potential sources for grants and scholarships.

Graduate schools, like undergraduate ones, do have some financial aid packages which you should investigate. One of the best all-around resources is the Financial Assistance for Library and Information Studies available online from the ALA at www.ala.org/ala/educationcareers/education/financialassistance/index.cfm.[1] Arranged alphabetically by state, and Canada and Puerto Rico as well, Section I lists financial assistance offered by state library agencies, state library associations, educational institutions, and local libraries. The amount, requirements, deadline for applying, and the contact information are all included. Most of these offer $1,000 to $3,000, but, if you are eligible, there are some bonanzas buried in the list.

Section II identifies "National and Regional Awards Offered in the United States and Canada." These include awards offered by the ALA, divisions within the ALA, Beta Phi Mu (International Library & Information Studies Honor Society) scholarships, and others. While lengthy, the document is not comprehensive. To ensure that you have covered all possibilities, check out the websites of the library association in your state and see if it has awards that are not in the directory. Be aware that some states have two associations—with school librarians having a separate one.

The Association for Educational Communication and Technology (AECT) also offers awards, at www.aect.org/Foundation/Awards/Awards.asp.[2] Realize that AECT scholarships are for NCATE (National Council for Accreditation of Teacher Education) schools, while those from the ALA are for schools it accredits. Awards from state school library associations usually are for either type of institution.

Finally, one of the best sources for all types of funding is produced by the Foundation Center. Their Foundation Directory Online gives you the widest access to grant makers at http://foundationcenter.org/findfunders/funding sources/fdo.html.[3] You do need to subscribe, so check with your local public library to find the best place to access it. One of the reference librarians can direct you to the nearest site. Some foundations offer scholarships for women returning to the workforce. Others are interested in encouraging minorities to advance their education. While these possibilities are fairly obvious, grants and scholarships are given for so many different (and occasionally bizarre) reasons, it is well worth investigating. Having a librarian familiar with the Foundation Online Directory is a big help in finding some of the more unusual ones.

Show Me the Money

1. Based on the library schools you are considering, what will be your approximate costs?
2. Are you eligible for any scholarships listed in the ALA online directory?
3. What scholarships are available from the school library association in your state?
4. Can you get access to the Foundation Grants Directory? Is any assistance available to you?

ASKING YOUR ADMINISTRATOR FOR HELP

An elementary principal once said to his librarian, "Either you are the expert, or I am." That is a sobering statement for someone new to the field. The expectation is that you know what you are doing—or you are incompetent. Administrators do not realize that many aspects of your job were not covered in your coursework, and while you probably had a field experience of one hundred-plus hours, you did not get to see everything.

The message from that principal's statement is, if you run to your administrator for every little thing, you will become "too much work," and that leads to not being rehired at the end of the year. Getting a mentor, as recommended in chapter 4, eliminates most of the problem, but there are times when you should be going to your supervisor. By knowing when and how, you demonstrate you are a leader and a team player.

You should go to your administrator for help when you have a plan that will improve student achievement in some way and need his or her support to speed the process. For example, if your principal or supervisor wants to see more technology integration and you are aware of a new resource that can guide students into thinking more deeply and creatively (a number of programs do that, from VoiceThread to SlideShare or concept-mapping such as Spider Scribe or Wise Mapping), propose a workshop for a grade level or subject. Ask for help in getting it on the schedule.

When you discuss this, keep your meeting brief. Do not tell an extended story. Focus on what the resource does (offer a brief demonstration that you have prepared in advance), why it would be a good fit for the proposed group, and what specific support you want. Scrupulously follow any directions or recommendations you are given. After the workshop, which the administrator might attend, send a thank-you note for the support. If he or she was not present, include a concise summary of how it was received and what follow-up you are planning.

In times of budget cutting, seek out your administrator for guidance on setting priorities. If the library budget is reduced significantly, choices about purchases must be made. Should all hard copies of magazines be eliminated, even though they appeal to reluctant readers? If you are considering not re-subscribing to some databases, how are you to choose between subject areas that will be affected?

Enter a meeting on making cuts with what the alternatives are and the cost of each. Discuss what you think is the best course, but explain you want to ensure that your priorities are aligned with those of the school and district. The benefits of reviewing options include making sure that the administration knows that there will be an impact, showing that you can analyze and make difficult decisions, and expanding your supervisor's understanding of the multifaceted aspects of your program and how these contribute to student learning.

If you have established a good working relationship with your supervisor, ask for help in bringing in a speaker on a topic of interest to the librarians for a professional development day. As discussed previously, most workshops address teacher needs. It probably has not occurred to the administration that the workshops typically offered are not directly connected to the library program.

Be prepared with the topic, the speaker, and the cost. By explaining why this presentation will be beneficial to librarians and therefore the students, you once again open up a dialogue on the value of the library program. If you have made a good case, your administrator should be able to either advise you on how to proceed or, better yet, do what is necessary for you.

> **Getting a Hand**
> 1. How do these types of requests for help differ from asking how to manage a difficult student?
> 2. Which of the examples best shows that you are a leader?
> 3. Which best shows you are a team player?
> 4. Which best shows the value of the library program?

RUNNING EVENTS

Why would you want to run an event? It takes a lot of work and time. It rarely is part of your job description. However, events that even loosely connect to your program are an opportunity to showcase the library, involve you with others in the educational community, and, as a result, help you grow your career.

One of the simplest events to have in the library is a book fair. The tie to your program is obvious since you promote lifelong reading. Usually book fairs are held at the elementary and sometimes middle school level. Most often the parent/school association is already in charge of it. The chair of the event, or perhaps the principal, will contact you to tell you the dates the library's ordinary operations need to be closed. You can decide this gives you time off to catch up on your work, or you can be more proactive and get directly involved. When the books come in, see what is there. While award winners will have their medals printed on the cover, check titles against lists of notable books from the Association for Library Services to Children (ALSC) (www.ala.org/ala/mgrps/divs/alsc/awardsgrants/notalists/index.cfm). Print out a few copies of the list and have them on hand for volunteer parents.

While waiting for classes to come and make their selections, engage parents in a discussion about how they can promote the reading habit at home and what you are doing with their children to build information literacy. This is a simple community outreach that gets you recognized in a positive way. Of course, you will also help students as they browse the books on display.

A more complicated event on the same theme is to hold an author visit. This requires coordination with the administration as well as the parent/teacher organization that will subsidize the costs. (If that is not an option, you can apply for a grant from the local education foundation.) Do some research first to find names of authors who have had successful visits and learn the cost of such an event. Sometimes you can reduce fees by joining with another school. Query your state association's electronic discussion list for recommendations. You will get a good working list back—and also the names of the contacts at the publishers with whom the event must be scheduled.

Well in advance of the visit, introduce the author's works to students and have them generate a list of questions they would like to ask him or her. Getting familiar with the different tittles helps them decide which one or ones they wish to purchase. The exercise teaches students to delve more deeply into the books and go beyond questions such as "How much money do you make?" Keep students' names next to their questions.

Arrange to have parents present the day of the event to help with the classes coming to meet the author. Keep the process as simple as possible by having students purchase their books several weeks before the visit to ensure they are on hand on the big day. Put their names and that of their teacher on a sticky note. (For those who buy a few of the author's works, keep them together with a rubber band.) This allows the author to do the signings before students arrive. The parents can help distribute the books as students enter. Invite your volunteers to join you and the author for lunch.

Have teachers put name tags on students so parents can easily hand out the books and the author can see these when speaking to the children. Give students the questions they generated earlier. This will get the dialogue started and remind them about thoughtful questions. Of course, the author's talk may raise other ones and be sure students feel free to ask these.

Author visits are more infrequently held at the high school level, usually in conjunction with one or more English teachers. At this level you might also work with a creative writing teacher to hold an evening "Poetry Slam" with a great display of poetry books that can be checked out that night. (There is something special about borrowing books from the school library at night.)

Another possibility includes hosting a legislative day or evening together with social studies teachers. Students do research in advance so their questions are relevant and recognize the political positions taken by these leaders. Parents should also be invited and volunteers can bring light refreshments for the end of the program.

Organizing and preparing for an event is another place to ask for help from your administrator. Most often what you are looking for is permission and support. You will get both more readily if you can connect the event to student learning.

For all of these events, inform the local media (with administrator approval). They tend to be willing to come when students are doing something because it sells newspapers or brings viewers to local news programs. Prepare a fact sheet about the occasion so reporters know what to expect and have the correct spelling of the names of people involved. Once their presence is confirmed, be sure to inform and invite your principal, supervisor, and superintendent of schools.

Because the library is an ideal gathering place, numerous events are scheduled there, from board meetings to inductions into honor societies and various other functions. Although you are not responsible for these and probably will not be present, they are taking place in your "home." You may feel that a "neat" library is an unused one, but visitors are not likely to think the same way. Make sure all visible desk areas are orderly and the facility looks welcoming to guests.

Where you can make connections to the event, set up a display of books on the topic with a handout of the bibliography along with suggested websites. You may not be there, but this makes your presence felt and demonstrates the importance of the library program to the intellectual life of the educational community.

Sponsoring and Hosting Events

1. How would you approach your principal to get support for an event?
2. Select an event and explain how it promotes student learning and the library program.
3. List the ways sponsoring an event helps you grow your career.
4. If you held an author visit via Skype, what additional strengths would you be demonstrating?
5. What did you learn about the benefits of running an event?

BASICS OF BUDGETING: FOUNDATION FOR ADVANCEMENT

Unlike teachers, you are responsible for preparing a budget for your program. At the elementary level, it may be only a few thousand dollars (and at times during the economic downturn it can be virtually nothing), while a high school budget tends to run into the tens of thousands, although it, too, is less than it was. Whatever it is, do not be intimidated by the process. What you learn as you go along will be invaluable.

Shortly after the start of school, you will be given a date when your budget for the *next* year is due, usually accompanied by forms (print or online) to complete and, hopefully, copies of the previous year's allocations. If you are not given this, check the files in your office for the information. You need it in any case to know what you have left to spend (most will have been expended at the end of last year).

High school librarians generally work from the same budget structure as administrators. That is, their expenditures are divided into several line items. One line would include all the books, periodicals, videos, and software. Another might be for contracts such as maintenance on a security system.

Purchases of online databases can be part of the line item for books or it could be a separate one.

Check the information you have to see if you are expected to purchase office and library supplies ranging from bulletin board paper to book pockets to ink cartridges. In some districts it is included in your budget. Other places allow you to get your materials from the general school supply. If the latter is the case, you still might be asked to submit a list of what you anticipate needing. Base your estimate on what was ordered the previous year, and then monitor what you use to see if what you requested matched your needs.

In the past, secondary school budgets had a line item for professional development which was used for conference attendance and, sometimes, dues in organizations. This is rapidly disappearing as budgets become more constricted. Many high schools have a separate, if relatively small, budget line for professional materials—books and periodicals for teachers. Capital expenditures which cover the cost of large items such as renovations and remodeling are handled separately and are also becoming rare.

In preparing your budget for the next school year, be guided by what was done in the past. You can tweak it to strengthen an area that you think needs it—for example, planning to extend the collection of graphic novels (being sure that you have a good rationale for your decision and clear it with your administrator). Be cautious about making too many changes until you have a better grasp of your expenditures and the needs of students and teachers.

Elementary librarians most often are told how much money they have and are expected to allocate it wisely, but may not get to see the line items. Since budgeting occurs early in the year, just follow directions. However, ask the high school librarian if you can have a copy of that budget for your own information. The size is usually eye-opening to those at lower levels, but your purpose is to learn what it looks like.

At all levels, try to get a copy of the district budget for the current school year. (You are working on the next year.) See how the library fits within the school's allocations. If at all possible, go to meetings where the board explains the proposed budget to voters. You can tell what is valued by how it is funded. Even when there are heavy cuts, some programs will feel it less than others.

Learning what the district values is important information for your future. In order to successfully propose changes, you must be aware of the larger picture, not just focused on what you need. Framing your planning to align with the direction your administration wants to take the district will advance your career and the library program.

Understanding how the budget is constructed, knowing what is included in each line item, and how monies may be moved within and between line items gives you the background to use your funds most effectively. Your building secretary can help you through the process of shifting within your budget.

Particularly at the high school level, you might check with the accounts payable person in the central office.

Budgets are most instructive when viewed longitudinally. After you have been in the district a few years, you will be able to see patterns. Which departments or areas suffer the worst cuts? Try to figure out the reason. It could be anything from how funding comes from the government and state to personality issues. The reasoning process is the same for favored areas. Once you have determined probable factors for the allocations, consider how you can use this information to strengthen what the library program receives. If you remain a building-level librarian, having a solid understanding of the budget process will help your program. If you move on to more administrative duties, the knowledge will benefit your career.

Budget Basics

1. Ask elementary, middle, and high school librarians for copies of their current budgets. (You may need to promise to keep it confidential.) Compare the three as to size, what is and is not included, and whether the line item (account #) is obvious.
2. What conclusions can you draw?
3. What, if anything, surprised you?
4. Were the librarians willing and able to discuss their budgets with you?

PROTECTING YOUR JOB IN A POOR EMPLOYMENT ENVIRONMENT

If you focus on "protecting your job," you will not be successful. Protection is a defensive attitude. Mentally, you are pulling up the drawbridge and trying to secure your castle against those who would raze it. That is not an inviting picture.

What is necessary is for you to create a strong advocacy program that is designed to make the library program vital to stakeholders. In designing it, keep as a guiding principle this concept: *how you are valued is more important than how valuable you are.* You know what you do is invaluable to students and teachers, but that does not matter unless *they* value it.

So how do you get others to feel you and the library program are too valuable to lose? Have a plan. Start small until you build your relationships and your reputation. Fortunately, you do not have to create an advocacy strategy on your own. Go to "Issues &Advocacy" on the AASL website at http://aasl.org/ala/mgrps/divs/aasl/aaslissues/issuesadvocacy.cfm for a variety of resources from which you can choose. Definitely sign up for the "Advocacy Tip of the Day." Keep a file of these. Use the ones you are most comfortable with at first. As you become more confident, you can try the more ambitious ones. Best of all, each day brings a new idea.

There are several toolkits at the site with which you should become familiar. The two most important ones are the "School Library Program Health and Wellness Toolkit" (www.ala.org/aasl/aaslissues/toolkits/slmhealthandwellness) and the "Parent Outreach Toolkit" (www.ala.org/aaslissues/toolkits/parentoutreach), which provide the resources for building an effective advocacy program. Too many librarians turn to this page when they need the "Crisis Toolkit" (www.ala.org/aasl/aaslissues/toolkits/crisis). Since that one is designed for when cuts are about to be announced, much of your efforts are expended in trying to gain support even as plans are being made to reduce or eliminate your position and program. At this stage, your actions come from desperation and you are less effective. Far better to be proactive and develop partnerships that will be firmly in place if and when there is talk of cutting school library positions.

In developing your advocacy program, keep in mind that the most powerful stakeholders are the administrators and the Board of Education. Throughout the school year, bring the value of the library to them. Remember to present the information in ways that *they* see as valuable. Student achievement and scores rank high for them. Do not just *tell* them, *show* students at work. An extremely effective communication to your administrators and the board is to create videos (use Vimeo, www.vimeo.com, or Animoto, www.animoto.com) or try a magazine format using Issuu (http://issuu.com) showcasing the highlights of the month, quarter, or as an end-of-the-year report. This will get far more attention than a lengthy text account, and will highlight your ability to incorporate technology into your program.

Always be a team player as well as a leader. Never whine or be part of a group that constantly finds fault with what the administration is doing. When a plan of yours is blocked for some reason, look for an alternative means of achieving it and propose it to your principal. If money is the issue, find a grant. Your local education foundation is one source. See what community support you can get for it. Be creative and *very* visible, and work with the other librarians in the district to do the same. Cuts are usually across the board, so *all* of you need to be viewed as invaluable for the library programs to be sustained.

> **Preventative Maintenance**
>
> 1. Besides the three AASL toolkits mentioned, which others do you think will be helpful in building a strong library program?
> 2. Which idea in the Parent Outreach Toolkit do you think you will definitely use?
> 3. Which of the "Quick Tips" in the School Library Program Health and Wellness Toolkit are you likely to try?

KEY IDEAS

- Plan to learn something from any district professional day no matter how far removed the workshop might seem from what you do.
- Suggest, in conjunction with other librarians in your district, specific workshops aligned with the library program for future professional days.
- Attend webinars and conferences (virtually or in person) to continue your professional development.
- Take online courses (or choose something from the AASL e-Academy).
- Join national organizations such as AASL, ISTE, and AECT, and read their journals.
- Read professional books over the summer.
- Go for a master's degree if you do not have one.
- Determine whether you wish to attend only an ALA-accredited school or would consider an NCATE-accredited program.
- Check ALA's Financial Assistance for Library and Information Studies for potential scholarships and grants.
- Find out if your state's school library association offers any scholarships.
- Access the Foundation Grants Directory, with help if possible.
- Ask for help from your administrator in a way that strengthens your program and keeps you as the expert, such as getting support for a plan that will improve student achievement.
- Running a successful event makes your program visible and valuable.
- Know the library budget history.

- Become familiar with the district budget and see how the library programs fit within it.
- Use AASL resources to develop a strong advocacy program.

NOTES

1. American Library Association, "Financial Assistance for Library and Information Studies," www.ala.org/ala/educationcareers/education/financialassistance/index.cfm.
2. Association for Educational Communication and Technology, www.aect.org/Foundation/Awards/Awards.asp.
3. Foundation Center, "Identifying Funding Sources: Foundation Directory Online," http://foundationcenter.org/findfunders/fundingsources/fdo.html.

6

POLISHING YOUR SKILLS

Never think you have come to the end of your journey. There is always more to learn, more to do, and much more to achieve. Begin by discovering how to manage your administrators, a key element in getting their support for your endeavors. Increasingly, you will lead others and this requires you to know how to create a climate that encourages these people to produce. However, to head a team, you must first understand how to be a trusted team member.

Improve the skills that will allow you to bring your message to the forefront. Increase the ways you venture outside the district, enabling you to bring back your experiences, implement new practices, integrate the latest technology, and translate trends in pedagogy into your teaching while skillfully helping teachers incorporate them as well. In so doing, you become more than just an instructional partner and move toward being an educational consultant. In this role you are a recognized resource for teachers and may fulfill a similar function for administrators as well.

MANAGING UP

Many will tell you that "managing up" is much more difficult than "managing down." As a school librarian, you have little practice in doing either, but both are important for your career advancement. If you are a solo librarian, your only opportunity to manage down is with volunteers, but no matter what your situation, you can always manage up.

Managing up is just what it sounds like. You manage your administrators. But before you step back from the concept, understand that this is neither brown-nosing nor manipulating. It means becoming a right hand as well as a team player. You have already been developing the necessary skill set for dealing with all your supervisors, now take it to the next level.

To manage your administrator you must know what he or she wants and needs. Active listening is critical here because few people spell these out specifically. You want to determine what aspect of the educational program is most important to her. Is she heavily committed to STEM (science, technology, engineering, and mathematics) or is literacy her big issue? No matter which area of the curriculum is her prime interest, your program can add to it. Find opportunities to show her what you can contribute.

Maintain a positive attitude and be seen as a team player. By being someone your principal can count on, you become a trusted ally. (Of course, you *never* use this position to carry tales or speak negatively of your colleagues.) A *Wall Street Journal* article recommends that you keep superiors informed. You can call attention to the library program while praising the use of it by teachers.[1] Remember not to blindside her either. No matter how serious the issue, not informing an administrator is far worse than avoiding bringing it to her attention.

Be solution-oriented. Instead of referring to something as a problem, discuss it as a challenge and offer at least one solution. Your principal may not take it, but that provides a basis for a dialogue and keeps you from sounding like a whiner.

Recognize and work with your administrator's style. Some like e-mails; others prefer memos and reports, and some like "chats." Whatever her preference, that is the way you must communicate. Also be aware of *how* to bring issues. You must be cognizant of how to phrase your messages. Most busy principals want you to be as succinct as possible, but there are those who want the underlying dynamics.

Once you have mastered these basics of managing up, broaden your scope. While your principal is the head of the building, she is one cog in the larger educational system. Keep your eyes and ears open to learn how she is perceived by her superiors. What does she need to do to impress them? How can you assist her in achieving that?

By seeing your principal in the larger setting you begin to see the bigger picture as it applies to you. From your perspective the library program is of exceedingly high importance. On a district level, it must fit into other challenges and demands. This does not mean you will not be promoting your program, but rather that you articulate your ideas in a manner that shows you understand the issues facing administrators.

For example, in a time of extreme budget cutbacks, you need to frame the discussion in terms of ROI (return on investment) and cost savings. Your underlying message is that libraries give the district the biggest bang for the buck. Just be careful not to undercut teachers in presenting your ideas.

Being truthful and having integrity are crucial. As noted earlier, managing up is neither brown-nosing nor manipulation. If you principal comes up with an idea that you do not think will work, say so. Focus on the issue she is trying to address. Frame your response to show why the results may not be what she is intending and suggest a different approach. If you think the whole idea is not a good one, have a discussion centering on whether this is the best investment of time and resources. The bottom line is that you do not lie, and you do not by silence give your agreement to something you believe will not work or is wrong.

Ever Upwards

1. Which of the skills you have acquired so far will help you in managing up?
2. What do you think is the greatest challenge in managing up?
3. Knowing yourself, what will you need to work on to successfully manage up?

BEING A TEAM PLAYER

Numerous references throughout this book have been made to being a team player. However, the practice is so important that it warrants special focus on just how to do it. The support you get from administrators rests heavily on whether or not they perceive you as a team player.

You have a choice in how you view and work with the administration. If your attitude is "they have forgotten what it is like to be in the trenches," or "they kowtow to parents and ignore what teachers know," you will be in constant confrontation. Faculty members who feel this way cannot be openly insubordinate, but they exhibit passive/aggressive behavior towards whatever initiative is introduced. While complying to the degree that they must, they let their colleagues know this will never work and drag their feet as much as possible, doing what they can to make their prophecy come true. Meanwhile, they make negative comments about the plan and the administrators behind it.

In general, these naysayers are not usually the best teachers, but they often attract a like-minded group. In places where enough teachers fall into this camp, any change has a difficult uphill battle. Unfortunately, negative comments tend to be fun to repeat, and since the library is an easy place for teachers to hang out and gossip, you need to be particularly careful not to get drawn into this behavior.

Team players are those who understand that for a school to succeed at educating students, everyone must be successful. Working together and helping each other is the best way to achieve this. The old saying "There is no 'I' in team" is at the core of what you should be projecting as you interact with teachers and administrators.

Maintain an open attitude towards whatever program or plan is introduced. Learn what is motivating it. Just as great athletes always know what is going on everywhere in the game, so do team players in a school understand the larger picture. Not only should you seek to understand what is happening in the building, you should also be looking at the district and even the state to see how it all fits in.

Once you recognize underlying and overarching issues, you are better able to focus on the key aspects of the plan. For example, in one high school the administration promoted block scheduling. While losing favor now, this approach doubled the length of class periods. Students either alternated the subjects on their schedule from one day to the next, or, in the more extreme version which required additional tweaks, students would have half their schedule one semester and the other half the following one. Although teachers were encouraged to provide input, were given time to visit other locations to see it in action, and much professional development was offered to train faculty, what was obvious was that this was a done deal no matter what the faculty thought. The administration was committed to the change before introducing it.

Feeling the new plan was being forced on them, even good teachers became resentful. Panic and resistance were a constant theme whenever teachers got together. However, the librarian was listening hard to what the administrators were saying. The concern was that lectures were the predominant teaching method in too many classes. No teacher would attempt to do that for the ninety minutes of the new longer class periods. Heavy-handed as it was, what the administration wanted was to change the method of instructional delivery.

By focusing on that need, the librarian quietly worked with teachers, acquiring materials (and getting extra funding to do so) that would give faculty members specific tools and ideas for changing their teaching methods. She suggested that research projects would help and the expanded length of class periods would help students be more successful. By becoming a resource in a time of stress, the librarian proved invaluable to teachers. But equally important, in so doing, the administration saw her as a team player. Although not everyone was happy, the actions of the librarian made the transition to the new schedule smoother.

In another situation, a librarian had just completed a renovation of her facility designed to increase both floor and shelf space when she was told that the "School to Work" advisor needed to be given a section of the library because there was no other available location in the building. Once again, the decision was already made. The choice was in the librarian's reaction.

While she wanted to protest and complain, she realized that would not bring about any change in plans. Her next thought was to make the situation as unpleasant as possible for the advisor in hope that everyone would recognize how unfair this was and perhaps make the advisor so uncomfortable he might find an alternative. On further consideration, she recognized that such behavior would make her own work situation stressful and was counter to the library's mission of being a welcoming environment for engaging in knowledge-building activity. Instead, she worked to create an area that gave the advisor space to meet with students but still was integral to the library.

The advisor, who was an expert at writing grants, was so pleased that he had all the tech products he obtained added to the library's holdings. In addition, his purchases of occupational materials came from his budget and grant money but were cataloged as part of the library collection. He became a strong advocate for the program, and the students he saw became comfortable working in the library. The administrators were delighted with the librarian's method of handling the situation and viewed her as someone who steered rather than rocked the boat.

As with managing up, being a team player does not mean you are a sycophant or a doormat. You always stand up for your program, but you look for solutions rather than digging in your heels. For example, a large library back room used for storing periodicals was turned into an office for the history department when the central administration was temporarily housed in the school. The librarian used the situation to get rid of many of the back issues because students preferred to access magazines using the online databases, while she took advantage of the proximity of the history teachers to promote new collaborations. When the central administration returned to their building, the history department went back to their old quarters. It was obvious that the room would not be returned to the library. Rather than wait and see what would be done, the librarian consulted with the computer teacher across the hall and proposed the teacher move into the soon-to-be vacated space, and have the science department reclaim the room that was originally theirs.

The idea received support from the science department chair and the computer teacher who preferred the new location. The library gained a large lab and the active help of another tech-savvy person. Classes scheduled into the lab often spilled out into the library for print material and those in the library could often get additional computer access in the lab. The solution was beneficial to all.

By being proactive, the librarian improved her program instead of merely coping with whatever idea the administration devised. Mary Kay Ash has said, "There are four types of people in this world: those who make things happen, those who watch things happen, those who wonder what happened, and those who don't know that anything happened."[2] Who do you want to be?

> **Yay, Team!**
> 1. Why is it so important to understand the bigger picture?
> 2. How do you support administration decisions without alienating teachers?
> 3. Which anecdote was most enlightening for you?

IMPROVING YOUR COMMUNICATION SKILLS

Leaders excel at communicating, and to be positioned for advancement you do need to demonstrate leadership. (You also need to do so for the many other reasons previously discussed.) While you may think you write and speak well, the level at which you do so can always be improved.

Clarity in communication is essential. Read e-mails and other messages you have received from administrators and those you perceive as leaders. Analyze them to determine how quickly they got to the point. How readily could you ascertain what was important and what you were being told or asked to do? You probably will notice that some of these were not very clear. You had to make some assumptions—which may or may not have been correct.

Brevity is no guarantee of clarity but neither is a longer missive. Although the problem is not new, the ease of sending an e-mail or memo often means it gets written virtually in stream-of-consciousness. Time is of the essence, so a quick reread, if that, is the most that happens before the message is sent out. Too often, a follow-up is necessary to clarify any confusion caused by the first communication. That neither saves time nor promotes confidence in the sender.

If you want to be regarded as a leader and be taken seriously, think before writing and rethink before sending any messages. Consider why you are contacting this person or persons. What do you want them to know or to do? Until you become highly skilled at this, even if it is an e-mail, always put it in word processing first. Bullet points, either included or implied, help the reader understand what you are trying to say. If multiple items are covered, it helps to use words such as "first" and "finally." Of course, you should proofread, and hopefully your word processing program will pick up any spelling errors, which is the benefit of not typing your message directly into an e-mail.

Until you feel secure with your ability, when the recipient or the communication is important, ask a friend to read it and tell you what it says. You may be surprised to discover that you were not as clear as you thought. Also have them assess the tone of the message. Without realizing it, you may sound whiny or imperious. If you are contacting someone of a different gender, have your reader be the same sex as the recipient. Men and women do not react the same way to a message. You might be astonished at what you learn.

Oral communication skills are more difficult to master. You speak all the time with little time for reflection. Unlike with a written message, you cannot go back and fix it before it is sent. The active listening ability you began developing will be helpful here. Find a role model, someone who speaks with clarity. Identify what makes him or her so easy to understand.

Recognize the different skill set between speaking to someone directly and addressing a group. In the first instance, you can easily see the reaction of the listener and it is simple for that person to immediately ask for clarification. As an educator, you probably do not have any fears about standing in front of a class, although assessing your clarity is more difficult than with a one-on-one situation. If you have to address parents or other groups, the common fear of speaking to an audience may kick in. Preparation and experience will help you become more comfortable when faced with that challenge.

Be mindful of speech hesitations and "fillers." School yourself to avoid saying "uh" when you are talking to someone. Many people insert "you know" or "actually" or other phrases that have no meaning in context. They are habits. When speaking before a group, those speech patterns become annoying to listeners. Because they have become so ingrained, you may not be able to hear yourself using them. Have someone you trust pay attention to how you speak and let you know when you are using filler words.

Record yourself as you speak to a class. Play it back as though you are the student. Did everything make sense? Would you have had to make assumptions or were the key points clearly delineated? What improvements could you make?

> **Sending a Clear Message**
> 1. How would you rate your written communication skills on a scale of 1 to 10?
> 2. Is it the same for all methods of written communication?
> 3. How would you rate your oral communication skills in one-on-one conversations?
> 4. How would you rate your oral communication skills before a group?
> 5. What steps will you take to improve your skills?

IMPROVING COLLABORATION AND TEAMWORK

Leaders are skilled at collaboration. If you want to advance and be perceived as valuable, you must develop working relations with your colleagues. At the elementary level this is a particular challenge since in most locations students are dropped off at your door and the teacher departs. You will need to consciously work to make the connections that integrate you and your program into the classroom. Not only is this important as a step towards leadership, it is vital for your survival.

Too many elementary librarians thought that their jobs were secure because they provided contractual duty-free time for teachers. The economic downturn showed the error of their thinking. When cuts needed to be made, in numerous locations the faculty had no awareness of any contribution the school librarian made to student achievement. What the librarian did was so separate from what occurred in the classroom, no one knew or cared what happened once the students were in the library.

Although high school and most middle school librarians see classes only when teachers are present, collaboration—and therefore being viewed as vital—does not always occur. You will still need to be proactive in working *together* with teachers, developing units where your unique contribution is an integral part of the lesson or unit as well as reaching out to faculty members who do not use library resources with their students. Having a class come in with the teacher but without your involvement gives your program no greater respect than that of the elementary librarian who is seen as only covering duty-free time.

The challenging question is, how do you develop collaborative units? The answer has been implied throughout. First you must build a relationship with teachers. They have to know and trust you in order to be open to the idea of working with you. In general, teachers are solitary performers. They do not "play well with others." When the classroom door is closed, they are in charge of their domain. This attitude has been slowly shifting as younger faculty members accustomed to the group interactions of social networking prefer a collaborative style, and the increase in professional learning communities in many districts is encouraging even more traditional teachers to be open to collaboration. (For those unfamiliar with professional learning communities, websites such as this one from Public Schools of North Carolina will get you up to speed: www.ncpublicschools.org/profdev/resources/proflearn.)

Nonetheless, teachers need to know you in order to work with you. Look for means to bring them in. Food has always been a draw. Couple it with an after-school display of new resources both print and online. As they browse through what you have prepared, present a low-key sales pitch on how these can be utilized in a research project for which you would be glad to provide assistance ranging from gathering materials to teaching and developing ideas for unit-ending multimedia presentations by students.

Another technique is to put items relating to a teacher's personal or professional interest in his or her school mailbox—or e-mail articles when appropriate. Whatever the method for this personal service, include a brief message. What you are doing is showing the teacher you are aware of what is of importance to him or her. The "high touch" approach usually brings a positive response.

You also need to develop relationships with students. Not only do you want them to be willing to listen to your advice, but also teachers are reluctant to have you work with their students if they sense that you are not at ease with them. Trust has to be built between you and teachers and between you and students to create a climate for collaboration.

Whether you are an elementary, middle, or high school librarian, you must be the proactive one if you want to work collaboratively with teachers. At the elementary level, be familiar with the units being taught and when they occur. Offer your resources to support these. At first, you will do little more than that. The next step is to work "cooperatively," meaning that your lessons coordinate with what is being taught in the classroom. You may not progress much from there, especially if your day is filled with scheduled classes. If it isn't, you might be able to do some mini-projects with the teacher present.

At the middle and high school level, offer to do brief workshops at department meetings. These can result in units first conceived as part of your presentation. Always keep looking for new opportunities to connect with teachers and their curriculum. Identify faculty members and departments who do not use the library and develop strategies to lure them in. The initial concept should be limited, nothing overwhelming. Small steps will bring you to your goal.

How you collaborate on your first joint project will determine whether you will be able to build on this initial step. You must be able to fit into the teacher's style. If he or she is detail-minded, every "i" must be dotted and every "t" crossed before you begin. Incorporate checklists for the two of you as well as the students so the teacher feels assured that everything is on track. Someone whose style is much looser is likely to be willing to "go with the flow," which can be challenging if you prefer to have responsibilities clearly spelled out.

No matter the teaching style, be clear as to what students are expected to produce (you can make lots of suggestions here), what will be required as part of the final presentation, and if you will be responsible for any of the grading. A debate rages constantly as to whether librarians should evaluate students, since it is healthy for them to have one place in the building that does not assign grades. Elementary librarians who must prepare report cards because they are the sole teacher for their classes sometimes choose to mark students based on attitudes rather than specific skills. When doing collaborative projects, you might want to take on assessing the bibliographies. While you are still grading, it is only a small portion, is related to what you teach, and tends to make students listen to you more attentively.

Do make every effort to be present when final presentations are given. Seeing these is necessary for you and the teacher to evaluate the project and see where it can be improved. It also sends a message to students that you are an integral part of the teaching process.

Working Together

1. What do you perceive as the most challenging aspect of creating a climate for collaboration?
2. Which of the proactive suggestions is most natural for you? Do you have any other ideas?
3. What is your teaching style? Have you been able to adapt your style when working with others?
4. How do you feel about giving students grades for their work in the library?

PRESENTING AT CONFERENCES

Take your communication skills to the next level by presenting a program at a conference, starting at the state level. Most state library associations have one each year. If yours does not, the state education association probably does. Check their online site to find out the date when the conference chair wants programs submitted. If you can partner with a teacher with whom you have worked, so much the better. You might even be able to do the presentation at both conferences, spreading the word on what librarians can bring to the classroom.

For your topic, look to a unit that worked particularly well. It should represent twenty-first-century learning with opportunities for students to use multimedia formats both for locating information and presenting their findings. The project should involve group work—possibly extending beyond your school—and require new knowledge to be constructed. Technology should be interwoven for accessing information, sharing, and presenting. Think about what the students liked most about the project. Be sure you have identified the underlying essential questions that framed the unit, and the enduring understandings that students took away.

Download the program proposal and work your way through it. Most provide guidelines which are helpful in developing the structure for your presentation. You will need to determine the length of the time slot you are requesting. Concurrent sessions usually are one to one and a half hours. Pre-conference workshops can be a half or full day. You probably do not want to take on something of that size the first time.

If you plan on a lecture format, one hour is a good length. However, the best programs require some audience participation. By engaging with the information, participants are more likely to remember the content and integrate it into their own practice. To have time for this, a ninety-minute slot is preferable.

Be mindful of the conference theme as you describe and title your program. If you want your proposal to be seriously considered, it must fit with the overall concept of the conference program committee. You might also be asked to identify the audience for your presentation. Is it targeted towards a specific grade range or years of experience? Tempting as it is to be all-inclusive, you do not want to lure attendees who will not benefit from your program. Either they will walk out, which is both disruptive and deflating for you, or they will give you a low rating on the evaluation sheets.

In preparing the proposal you usually are asked to outline the ideas and the sequence in which you plan to present them. You need some sort of opening that focuses participants on your topic, followed by its development, and a closing that has participants reflecting on what they learned and how they will use it. Some proposals ask for a short description which is printed in the conference program as well as a longer one that helps the committee decide whether to accept it. When completing an online form, it is easy to fill in the boxes as you go along, but take the time to write out everything in word processing before copying and pasting it in to the form. You want to be sure that you have chosen your words well, aligned with the theme, stayed within the word limit, and, of course, have no spelling or grammatical errors.

Once you have presented at your state conference a few times, consider doing it on the national level. An easy entry is offered by the AASL at its biennial conference. The opening "Exploratorium" is a giant poster session. You can even do this as your first attempt, since you will not have to deal with any stage fright. Here, you speak to a few people at a time as they approach your display and show interest. After a few groups have listened to your talk, any nervousness you might have felt at the beginning will disappear, and you will begin to have fun.

You may be surprised to discover that your audience (whether it is one person or ten) is impressed with your presentation. This will build your confidence and make it easier for you to do a program for larger groups. After doing a few of them, your speaking skills will improve as you develop fluency in presenting your ideas to others.

Expand your focus by doing presentations for various teacher conferences. Almost all academic subject areas have associations that put on a convention. If you did a unit with a science teacher, for example, find out when her state conference is, and submit a joint proposal. This way you are not speaking to the choir, but showing teachers how the librarian can be an instructional partner and improve student learning.

Always inform your administrators or supervisor when you are presenting a program or workshop. Provide them with the short description you submitted in your proposal. Follow up afterwards, letting them know how it went. When they are preparing end-of-the-year evaluations, make a point of sending them a list of your professional activities outside the building. Too often, librarians (and teachers) think of this as bragging and just hope the administrator might learn of it; however, unless you alert them to your contribution to the educational community, they will be unaware of it. This is one more way to demonstrate your value and the importance of your program. Additionally, you principal might appreciate the information since he or she submits regular reports to the superintendent, and this would be a positive item to include.

Stepping Out in the World

1. When does your state's library association hold its conference?
2. Download a conference proposal form and see how you might structure a program.
3. What experiences have you had in speaking before an audience?
4. Would you prefer to present on your own or with a partner?

IMPROVING PROJECT PLANNING SKILLS

Projects showcase your program and your leadership skills. Developing and improving your abilities in this area requires you to learn by doing. You have two options to get started. You can join a school or district committee charged with getting a task done such as creating a technology plan, revising or creating a curriculum, or preparing documentation for a visit from an accrediting agency, or you can design your own project.

The first alternative involves less risk, but you have fewer opportunities to demonstrate the value of your program or your leadership skills. On the other hand, if you have never been involved in carrying out a project, this is an excellent place to learn. The key to the success of the committee rests with the chair. Observe the chair's positive and negative behaviors as they affect both the project and the committee members.

At the first meeting, did the chair ensure that all members know something about each other and present a clear picture of the desired outcome? The tone set at the initial gathering affects everything that follows. It is vital that everyone feel connected to each other and know what is expected. This includes a discussion of how often, when, and where meetings will be held. A rough timeline should be presented and responsibilities assigned. Committee members should be able to suggest revisions to the timeline and volunteer for their individual tasks. An authoritarian approach precludes ownership by those involved and will lessen the quality of the final product.

As work gets underway, do you have a sense of it being organized and directed? Are there opportunities to share the various assignments with the larger groups? How well and how often does the committee chair communicate with members? Is feedback solicited and listened to? Are deadlines being met or is the project getting sloppy? Do you believe targets will be reached? Is the committee growing more or less cohesive? Is the chair open to revising the timeline and other changes when these seem necessary and appropriate?

When the project is completed, note how it is wrapped up. Is the presentation effective? Are all contributors recognized? Do all committee members have a sense of pride in what was achieved? Remember that you can learn almost as much from a poor performance as from a great one.

In developing your own project, start small but look for something that can easily be seen by others. One possibility is weeding a visible section of your collection. A big mistake novices make is to assume that if their project is small, they can plunge right in and make adjustments as they go along. Remember the truism, "if you fail to plan, you are planning to fail." Although all plans are subject to tweaking as the situation demands, you will always be more successful if you have a clear idea of where you want to go and how and why you want to get there.

Before launching any project regardless of its size, identify your goal. Do you just want to get rid of outdated material or are you also looking to increase shelf space for new acquisitions? Will this require extra funding and therefore support from the administration?

What will you use as your rationale? Using Follett's TitleWise program for collection analysis of that section will show its average age and how it compares with the recommended range.[3] Consider the resources you will use to determine what should be eliminated. *Less Is More* by Donna J. Baumbach and Linda L. Miller is an excellent, user-friendly source.[4] Whether or not you are seeking extra funds, you should make your administrator aware of what you plan. Obtain approval if necessary. Share your goal, your rationale, and the resources you will use as well as your plan for accomplishing the project.

If at all possible include others in the planning process. This will relieve you of some of the work, encourage ownership from different members of the educational community, and give you additional eyes and alternate perspectives. For example, you might think that as a professional, only you should weed the collection, but teachers have subject area expertise and might enjoy being part of the process. One shop teacher who had never used the library was flattered to be consulted about books being considered for withdrawal from the collection because they seemed outdated. While providing his knowledge of the subject, he discovered the library's holdings could contribute to his program.

Although you are the one to make the final decision, you can prepare guidelines and have books put on a cart for you to check before actual discarding. Explain whenever you choose to retain a title. Deleting the items from your catalog can also be done by others. Once you have learned your district's policy for removing materials purchased with taxpayer money, discuss the procedure with those on your team.

Develop a timeline defining the tasks to be accomplished, who will be responsible for doing each, and the planned completion date (and when appropriate the start date). Review all the steps with your team and ask for questions and comments. It is possible that you have overlooked something or were not clear about the process. Be open to making changes, which lets everyone know you value their work and their input.

Throughout the project keep everyone informed of its progress. With the weeding example, announce the current total of books deleted from the collection and their average age—or—if you have some ancient ones—some specific copyright dates. Mention any dated titles or obsolete information included. Congratulate any subgroups for accomplishments since your last report.

Prepare a report for your administrator summarizing the project and what was achieved, highlighting the contribution of all those involved. Circulate a draft version to your team, asking for comments, additions, and deletions. Respect what you are told and make changes accordingly.

POLISHING YOUR SKILLS

Once you have successfully completed a few small projects, you are ready to tackle a larger one such as a renovation, a major rearrangement of the collection, installing a security system, or migrating to a new automated system. Besides what you have done for your smaller plans, make this part of a strategic plan tied to your library mission or vision statements. You can have sub-goals for this as well as making sure your rationale involves a significant benefit to students and learning.

Your team in a major project is a critical component for its success. If you are doing a renovation, regard the clerk of the works or the general contractor as well as key subcontractors as part of your team, whether or not they are aware of it. Communicating with them, listening to what they tell you, and letting the appropriate people know if something is going wrong will reduce problems during construction and in the future. For example, a librarian noticed that somehow the electrical plans for the new workroom had only one outlet and the position of the floor outlet for the circulation computer was placed under the spot the desk was going.

Consider the accounts payable clerk as also on your team. This person will keep you abreast of the bidding process early in the project and, if you have established lines of communication, when invoices have been submitted for partial and final payments. You want to be sure that nothing is signed off until you have determined that everything has been done according to specifications.

Your staff, if you have one, or committed volunteers if you don't, is your core team. Depending on the project and the grade level you serve, students might also be part of the team and have input in the planning process since the outcome should be to serve them better. Teachers and parents are other candidates for the team.

How many people to include is dependent on the size of the project. More than ten will likely make it unmanageable unless you have some on the initial stage and others who come on board later. All members should develop a sense of ownership and commitment to what you are trying to accomplish. In addition to being extra sets of eyes, they can also be your voice in the community, letting other know the value of the project and how the library program serves student achievement.

Planning for Success

1. Name one or two school or district committees which would help you develop planning skills.
2. What are some small projects you can do to build your planning skills?
3. Who would you put on your team?
4. Besides renovating the library, what large project might you do?

KEY IDEAS

- "Manage up" by becoming a team player.
- Identify your administrators' wants and needs and work with their preferred communication styles.
- Be solution-oriented.
- Speak in "administrator language" to make your points.
- Be open to whatever new program or plan is introduced and discover the underlying motivation behind it.
- Stand up for your program, but do not be intractable.
- For written clarity, before sending a message, identify your purpose and what you want the recipient to know or do.
- Have a trusted colleague listen when you address a large group and then give you feedback.
- To develop collaborative partnerships, start by building relationships.
- Always be proactive.
- Fit your instruction to the teacher's style.
- Submit a proposal to present a program at a state or national conference.
- Inform administrators whenever you present a program or workshop.
- Learn project planning by joining a school or district committee charged with accomplishing a specific task.
- Start small when planning your first project.
- Be clear about the project's goals.
- When possible, include others in the project, beginning with the planning phase.
- Have a timetable for all aspects of the project, but accept that it will need adjustments along the way.
- Communicate the progress of the project to all stakeholders.

NOTES

1. Elizabeth Garone, "What It Means to 'Manage Up,'" *The Wall Street Journal: Careers Q&A*, October 30, 2008, http://online.wsj.com/article/SB122511931313072047.html.
2. Mary Kay Ash Quotes, www.famous-women-and-beauty.com/mary-kay-ash-quotes.html.
3. TitleWise Online Collection Analysis Questions, www.flr.follett.com/help/titlewise.html.
4. Diane J. Baumbach and Linda L. Miller, *Less Is More: A Practical Guide to Weeding School Library Collections*. (Chicago: American Library Association, 2009).

7
MOVING OUTWARDS

Here is where you take a big leap forward. In the last chapter, you were encouraged to take a risk by presenting at a conference. This was an initial step in moving beyond the security of your building and district and showing the administration that you can bring added value to the district. Become even more visible by continuing to reach outward.

Strengthen your leadership skills by first identifying the qualities that are needed and determine how well you are doing in developing them. Be aware of the importance of "emotional intelligence" in managing others. Another way to announce you are a leader and gain visibility for your program and recognition for your school is to become a National Board Certified Teacher-Library Media. Spread your wings by working with vendors, but be cautious about conflicts of interest.

DEMONSTRATING LEADERSHIP

Leadership and its importance to your career have been an ongoing theme throughout this book, and there have been numerous examples of how to develop the trait. However, many confuse leadership with a job title and somehow think they need to wait until they are called supervisors or principals. Administrators are said to be leaders because their title implies it. Yet everyone has had experiences with superiors who are exceedingly poor leaders. What is even less well known is that someone from the "ranks" can be a skillful leader. Although their colleagues may not consciously call them leaders, everyone recognizes these are the people who are seemingly behind and involved with every innovation that produces results. They are the ones to whom teachers turn when they have questions about almost anything relating to the job.

Once you take on this role, you will find that administrators value you as a key player, consult with you informally, and enlist your aid in their plans. In return, they support your projects, strengthening the library program. The growth of your program then furthers your development as a leader.

The goal is worth the effort, but what do you have to do to achieve it? You have already done much. The many professional development opportunities you have taken both in and out of the district have given you a solid knowledge base of new techniques and technologies as well as a growing understanding of the forces impacting school librarianship and education. Your observations of administrators have shown you what positive and negative practices look like. Now it is time to use your learning to expand your role and voice.

By this time you probably have outgrown your mentor, who might now be a trusted colleague. Rather than seeking out a new mentor for this next part of your career path, look for a role model. Is there a teacher in the building who is highly regarded by almost everyone? Is there an administrator who always gets support from faculty? These are the people you want to observe in action.

Next, consider the inner and exterior qualities great leaders have. Among the internal ones, first and foremost, they must have integrity. If they are not trustworthy, people will not follow them. It is too risky. Self-confidence is also necessary. It also inspires trust, since few would go along with someone who is always second-guessing every step and is uncertain of what to do next. Another attribute is being a visionary. Leaders are followed because they see a great future and know how to get there. The concept is exciting and inspires others to want to be a part of making it a reality.

Although not strictly a requirement, a sense of humor is always a good quality in a leader. Being able to laugh at yourself makes you more approachable. A good leader never uses humor to demean others. The underlying principle is to take what you do seriously and yourself lightly.

You have been working on several of the external qualities and now should take stock of how well you are doing on them. The first of these is being a good communicator. This means you can articulate what is needed with clarity, minimizing confusion, and you can speak persuasively. Clarity comes when you fully understand the direction you want to take and know what others can do to move it forward. While some can be convincing by throwing up a cloud of words, eventually the lack of substance shows through. To persuade others, you need to be fully knowledgeable about all aspects of the subject or project. In today's world you must have communication skills in a variety of formats. You need to be able to speak on your feet, write e-mails that are succinct and complete, blog purposefully, and, in many cases, post on Facebook and Twitter.

Good leaders also display empathy and know how to collaborate. Both involve strong people skills. Empathy means you can read body language and care about the lives and emotions of others. When you are empathetic, you do not start sharing your exciting new plans until you are certain your listener is in a place to take it in. If they are harried or upset, or are caught up in something wonderful happening to them, their attention is not on what you are saying. No matter how skilled a communicator you are, you will not get through. First, you have to listen, which is another trait of leadership. By letting the other person know you are interested in what is going on in their lives and giving them a chance to get it out, you create a space for your own plans to follow. One word of caution—do not try to fake empathy. Some administrators do this, and it is always seen as a form of manipulation.

Listening is also vital for collaboration. Everyone has had experiences with a superior who comes in with an idea, claims to want input, and then ignores any comments or ideas that do not go along with the original plan. You want people to "buy in" to what you are proposing and for that to happen, they need ownership.

For example, a librarian was planning a major renovation of the library. The big idea that had to be accepted was the renovation. Another piece of the renovation was that in order to maximize the available space, moveable stacks would be needed. The discussion focused on how the collection would be reorganized. The librarian had envisioned the fiction section as being located on the display-height shelving under the windows. One of the other staff members observed this would mean that the reference books would be moved and placed on high shelves and, considering the weight and size of some of them, would pose a danger and would not be as readily accessible as they should be. The librarian quickly realized the logic and value of the comment and plans were adjusted accordingly. As a result, the staff member who had some resistance to the new shelving was a far more willing partner in the renovation process. She had been heard and she could take pride in the contribution she made.

How then do you become a good—or great—leader? Knowing the qualities and attributes of a leader is the first step. Practice comes next. Begin with your strengths and look for avenues to polish them. Work on the areas in which you are weaker. This is where identifying a role model can be particularly helpful. Watch how they demonstrate these characteristics and try your hand at emulating them.

> **In the Lead**
> 1. Why is it important for you to be a leader?
> 2. Which qualities of a leader do you have?
> 3. Which qualities of a leader are not natural to you?
> 4. How will you become more comfortable with them?

TUNING IN TO YOUR EMOTIONAL INTELLIGENCE

The business world has recognized the importance of emotional intelligence (EI). Oddly enough, education and school librarianship, which are so dependent on relationships, have yet to focus attention on the subject. This may be partly due to the uncertainty as to whether EI is inborn or can be learned.

The concept has been around since psychologists Peter Salovey and John Mayer published an article entitled "Emotional Intelligence" in *Imagination, Cognitions, and Personality* in 1990.[1] Since then the field has exploded. Whether you do a Google search or check Amazon.com, the listings on this topic are extensive. Although you can plunge into the academic discussions or delve into books on business, you may get what you need from a brief overview and a basic understanding of what it is about.

Simply put, EI deals with "the ability to perceive, control, and evaluate emotions" which is broken down into four areas: "perceiving emotions," "reasoning with emotions," "understanding emotions," and "managing emotions."[2] A facility with each of these eases your interactions with teachers, parents, students, and administrators. When you have a well-developed EI, you are more likely to get the support you need and build collaborative relationships since much communication occurs on the emotional level, although you are not necessarily aware of it.

If you have been actively observing and listening, you are already improving your ability to perceive emotions. Body language and voice signal what is happening far more than words. For example, a principal with a very low EI entered a room where two teachers were engaged in a conversation, and blithely interrupted them. Not aware that what was under discussion was of great importance to one of the teachers, he never noticed that her arms were crossed tightly over her chest. Her legs were also crossed, and her foot was rocking impatiently. The longer he spoke the faster her foot moved, but he never acknowledged what to most people were obvious signs of tension, frustration, and growing anger. He was taken aback when she finally blurted out, "Could you please leave now and save this for another time?" While this is an extreme example of inability to perceive emotions, there are many times when you can save yourself much grief by being sensitive to where another person is emotionally.

By contrast, a librarian noticed a teacher who was walking with slumped shoulders and asked what was wrong. The teacher said it was her department chair, but the librarian, sensing that the unhappiness was too great to be caused by an administrator, suggested the teacher join her in the library for a cup of coffee (the pot was always on). When asked what was *really* wrong, the teacher disclosed a serious family problem. Naturally, this was kept confidential, but the bonds of understanding were forged at that moment. With that secure, it was easy later on to develop projects together.

Reasoning with emotions sounds like a contradiction in terms, but people respond to what they care about. It is why you make lessons relevant to students' lives. How you feel about something conditions your thinking. Those who believe they are good at a subject do better than those who have decided they are not. The old adage, "if you think you can or you think you cannot, you are right" is correct. It is emotions interacting with reasoning. If someone thinks of the library as a stodgy place filled with books and librarians as bun-wearing, shushing women, they are not likely to think of using it for assignments requiring any kind of technology to complete. While this is another extreme example, many administrators harbor something akin to that view. You need to work hard to change emotional reasoning as it is often embedded at the subconscious level. To effect such a change requires you to be exceedingly proactive and a visible leader.

Understanding emotions is a critical component of collaboration and leadership. When someone is angry, you tend to respond either offensively or defensively. Most often neither is the best way to react. Stop before you say anything and take time to first determine whether you are the true target. Something may have occurred to set the other person off. You cannot get to the root cause when so much emotion is coming at you. It may not even be any of your business. Instead, ignore the "delivery" and focus on the message. By staying calm and not letting yourself get dragged into the drama, you can resolve the issue on the table, and once that is handled you may learn what triggered the tirade.

In the event that you are the one responsible for generating the ire, remaining calm is still the best response. Do not defend yourself or blame someone else, no matter what the truth is. Focus on dealing with the issue and finding the best possible solution. A shouting match with charges and countercharges flying leaves wounds that take a long time to heal. You cannot afford to alienate anyone in the educational community. You are responsible for maintaining at least a professional relationship with everyone with whom you come in contact. It is part of your job requirements. Keep as your maxim, "do I want to be right, or do I want it to work?" knowing that if you are determined to prove you are right—it will not work.

While negative emotions cause the most problems, you also need to understand positive ones as well. People who are relentlessly upbeat may be concealing their true feelings. Smiles can mask negative attitudes. You cannot miss anger, but you can easily overlook these potential trouble spots. Always use your active listening and observing skills so that you are not caught unaware and can deal with problems simmering below the surface before they erupt.

Finally, having a high EI means that you can manage emotions. The ability is reflected not only in how you interact with the emotions of others but also in how you control your own. Frustration, anger, and hostility are part of human nature. Feeling that way is normal, but what you do about these emotions determines how successful you are as a leader. There is no one surefire method of moderating your emotional responses. For some, the tried-and-true "counting to ten" is enough to calm them down. Doing something physical is another method for eliminating the excess energy of those feelings. Meditation works for others. For some, journaling the emotion is a way to get to the root of it and offers the possibility of analyzing its true cause and possible solutions. Venting with a trusted friend, (preferably not in the district and not giving specifics such as names) can be another outlet. You need to find what works best for you.

How High Is Your EI Quotient?

1. What are three benefits of improving your EI?
2. Can you identify someone's emotion before they speak? Do you recognize it in their voice?
3. How do you deal with confrontation?
4. What is your best method for managing your own emotions?

NATIONAL BOARD CERTIFICATION

The National Board Certification of Teachers is a rigorous process by which teachers demonstrate their exemplary qualifications in their area of expertise. The concept is similar to that for doctors and accountants. Achieving board certification tells employers and colleagues that you are highly accomplished.

Obtaining certification takes time and money. Many states provide financial assistance for those seeking National Board Certification and some offer pay increases to successful candidates. By going to the website www.nbpts.org you can find out if your state offers funding and what scholarships may be available to you. The site also provides detailed information about what is required and how to apply. You, of course, would want to seek the one for Library Media: Early Childhood through Young Adulthood.

In addition to financial support, look for other resources to further your candidacy. Gail Dickinson has written *Achieving National Board Certification for School Library Media Specialists: A Study Guide*, which is an in-depth guide to the entire process.[3] Check with your state's school library association to find out who has achieved board certification and ask one of them to mentor you. The website also has links to more than thirty networks that help candidates.

To be certified as a National Board Teacher, you will have to prepare a portfolio of four classroom practices following the guidelines which you can find on the website, and take an assessment based on six exercises created by specialists in the field. The time and the cost involved are considerable but the benefits are worth the effort. The obvious advantage to becoming certified is that your administration will be aware that you are an exemplary librarian, but you receive far more than that. Some states accept the certification for licensure, making it simpler if you should move to a new location. You will also find that teaching and library colleagues will look to you for help and advice. In other words, this is a path to leadership.

Even more significant is your own professional growth. The extensive requirements for certification make you aware of all the components that go into being an outstanding librarian. Your preparation for the four portfolios and the assessment exercises builds your skills and competencies. No matter how good you are before you start, you will be much better when you complete the process. Those who have earned board certification are justifiably proud of their accomplishment and so identify themselves in their digital and print signatures.

Certified Accomplished

1. How long after beginning your career would you consider applying as a candidate for National Board certification?
2. What resources does your state offer to offset the cost?
3. What resources in your state are available to help you through the process?

REACHING OUT TO THE COMMUNITY

Going out to the community and bringing the community into the school is another way of leading. Although it is important, you need to tread carefully here. Speak with your administrator to learn what outreach is already in place. You might be able to join an existing project to raise your own awareness of the various groups within the district. This is particularly helpful if you are not a resident.

Some districts prefer that all such outreach be handled by the administrators. If so, you will be more limited. Consider some of the ideas presented here, and then discuss with your principal the ones you think would work best for your situation. The suggestions you propose might help your administrator be more successful and therefore reflect positively on you and your leadership. You might also join him or her in bringing the proposal to fruition.

The easiest outreach is with the public library. If you have not done so already, you should begin here. This rarely sets off an alarm with the administration. Exchange information on programs. Promote theirs on your website and have them do the same with yours. Invite the public librarians to visit your library and, particularly if you are not a resident, make a point of going to the public library after school. You should know your colleagues.

For high school librarians with a community or four-year college in their district, a connection here is invaluable. You can have a college librarian talk to juniors and seniors starting a research project as to what is required and expected of college freshmen. A field trip to a college library is an eye-opener for students. They are not only overwhelmed by the size and the disappearance of the familiar Dewey Decimal System, but are also astounded at the number of databases which they are expected to use in doing research.

Developing a relationship with the business community can bring big returns to the school and your program. Kiwanis and Rotary clubs meet during the day, making it difficult if not impossible for you to attend a meeting. However, if your principal is a member, perhaps he or she could arrange for one meeting to be held in the library. Ask for time to make a brief presentation. Use programs previously discussed, such as a short Animoto (http://animoto.com) video slideshow, or Vimeo (http://vimeo.com) video to highlight the twenty-first-century learning happening in your library. Be prepared to answer questions and provide a hands-on tour of your facility.

Encourage the business people attending to give back to the school. With the help of your administrator, think of what you would like them to do. It might be as simple as having them sign up to talk at career day. At the high school level, one or two representatives can speak with students about interviewing for jobs and what they look for in an employee. If the high school does not have internships set up with local businesses, this can be another avenue to pursue. Ask them what they are looking for from graduates that they are not seeing, and then seek ways to integrate those skills into your program and in other subject areas.

Consider creating a two-way connection with senior citizen groups. Although this does not always work, active, alert members can become volunteers in your library. Know that they do not want to contribute too much time as they tend to be leading full lives, so prepare to be flexible. In exchange, see if one of the service clubs in middle or high school is willing to undertake teaching tech to seniors. The generational span benefits both groups and can result in more support for the school budget from a segment of the population that often votes against it.

Find out what nonprofit organizations are in your district. A local historical society might be delighted to work with elementary social studies teachers or do something at the secondary level. If you have materials that are part of your school's history, you can offer to do a display at the museum. The local media are likely to cover it, giving you an opportunity to discuss how twenty-first-century school libraries serve students and the community.

See if the garden club would be willing to set up a floral or plant display in the library. Put your gardening books next to their contributions. Does the club encourage student membership?

What programs and services are offered to low-income families? Could you visit after school and do a story hour? Perhaps, with approval, they can have access to your online catalog. The district's internal delivery system might be able to bring books to their location on a weekly basis and pick up the items to be returned. School service clubs can collect current books (or raise money to purchase them) and slightly used tech, ranging from video games to computers, and contribute them. The object is for the school, the library, and students to become a true part of the community.

Community Connections

1. How open or resistant is your administration to reaching out to the community?
2. How would you begin a dialogue with your principal to suggest expanding community contacts?
3. Of the possibilities described, which do you think would be the best fit with your library program?

FOCUS GROUPS AND VENDOR ADVISORY BOARDS

If you have developed a good relationship with software producers or publisher representatives you might be asked to serve on a focus group. These are often set up at national and larger state conferences when vendors wish to see what is working or not working with one of their products or to see whether a new venture will be well-received. The group is usually small and, depending on the product, may consist of librarians from different fields.

After a presentation by one or more people from the company, you will have an opportunity to react. Often, the people selected are other high-performing librarians. Listening to their comments and getting to know them expands your own personal learning network. Share with your administrator that you were asked to be on a focus group and why.

The presentation itself is another avenue for you to grow. The vendor will be walking you through the product, showing its merits. Invariably you discover tricks, shortcuts, or capabilities you did not know about. When you bring this information to your teachers and students, they are likely to use the product more frequently, giving you a better return on your investment.

Most often, you join a focus group because the vendor contacted you, but you can try to volunteer. If you know a sales representative for a product you use, let him or her know of your interest. They are the ones the company asks for recommendations when they put a group together. In situations where you do not have a representative you see, suggest the possibility of your being on a focus group when speaking with customer service when you call or e-mail them concerning their product.

Becoming a member of a vendor advisory board is almost never discussed in library publications, possibly because proportionally few librarians do so. Yet there are many advantages to extending your professional expertise in this manner. Depending on your interest and connections, you might be asked to be on an advisory board.

Unlike a focus group which is a "one-shot deal," advisory board membership is more long-term. Some of the library automation system providers have them, as do vendors of the major software products. Frequently they meet at ALA conferences and you will get a free meal as part of the meeting.

You also will be contacted at various times throughout the year to provide input. On occasion, you might be asked to be a beta site or to go to a secured portion of their website and evaluate what is being considered for future enhancements. The vendor will have a prepared list of questions for you to answer regarding your thoughts. Having this contact gives you the opportunity to ask for changes that will be of help to you, your teachers, and your students depending on what the product is.

As with focus groups, serving on advisory boards brings you into contact with librarians outside your district. Hearing how they are using the product can give you ideas to incorporate into your program. Your conversations with them can also include other resources they like or lessons that have been particularly successful. Experiences such as these help you grow your expertise and your career far beyond what you could have done by just remaining in your school library.

> **The Vendor View**
> 1. Which sales representative might you speak with about serving on a focus group?
> 2. Ask your librarian colleagues if they serve on focus groups or advisory boards. What did they learn?

CONFLICTS OF INTEREST

The more you do beyond the walls of your school, the more you are at risk for conflicts of interest. You need to understand where the possible pitfalls are and how to avoid them. Usually when you think of conflict of interest, you are picturing some sort of bribe, but for people who are basically honest the danger is more subtle.

Some possible scenarios are very obvious. For example, if you are planning to change your automation system, it is an obvious conflict of interest to be taken to dinner by a vendor who is bidding on the new contract. However, if you are at a conference and the provider of the system you have in your library takes you (and others who own it) to dinner, you are probably not in violation. It should be noted that some places consider even that as a conflict because by attending you are endorsing their product or service.

It is a good idea to check with your administration to see if there is a district conflict of interest policy. In general, you need to be cautious of any remuneration. Some places put a limit on what may be accepted. For example, a twenty-five-dollar Starbucks gift card is usually not considered a problem, but if you receive much more you have undoubtedly stepped over the line. For some districts even the small gift card is not acceptable. In the absence of a policy, it is safest to report any gifts to your administrator and get approval for accepting it.

During holiday season, many companies send gifts, frequently food items, to their good customers. In some locations the administration might find it all right for you to share these with the staff. Where this is not acceptable, find out if you can donate it to a local charity and then inform the donor of what you did and why. You can feel secure in accepting pens, pencils, pads, and other small items with a company logo on them.

Do not let fear of conflict of interest deter you from reaching out beyond your school to build your career and leadership skills. Just be mindful of your district's guidelines and behave accordingly. When in doubt, do not accept a gift.

> **Avoiding Conflict**
> 1. Does your district have a conflict of interest policy?
> 2. Have you ever been given a gift by a vendor?
> 3. In light of what was discussed, do you think it was a conflict of interest?

KEY IDEAS

- You can and need to be a leader even though you are not an administrator or have a title that identifies you as a leader.
- External leadership qualities include integrity, self-confidence, vision, and a sense of humor.
- Internal leadership qualities include clarity in communication, collaborative work style, empathy, and being a good listener.
- Become a leader by carefully observing and learning from good and bad examples.
- A well-developed emotional intelligence is essential in gaining support.
- Know how to read body language.
- Respond to the message rather than the emotion while seeking to learn the true cause of an outburst.
- National Board Certification is time-intensive and expensive, but extremely beneficial to building your professional expertise.
- Learn what financial and mentor support is available in your state to those pursuing National Board Certification.
- Reaching out to the community builds support for your school and library program, but always check first with your principal.
- Public and academic libraries are an easy first step in community outreach.
- Work with your principal to reach the business community and seek to have it become a presence in your school and library.
- Find out what nonprofit organizations exist in your community and look for ways in which you can help each other.
- Being on a focus group expands your personal learning network and gives you insight into a product you use.
- Serving on a vendor advisory board gives you direct input into the future development of the product, making it a better fit for your teachers and students.
- Find out if your district has a conflict of interest policy and, if it does, follow it carefully.

NOTES

1. Peter Salovey and John D. Mayer, "Emotional Intelligence," *Imagination, Cognition, and Personality* 9, no. 3 (1989–90): 185–211.
2. "What Is Emotional Intelligence?—Definitions, History, and Measures of Emotional Intelligence," http://psychology.about.com/od/personalitydevelopment/a/emotional intell.htm.
3. Gail Dickinson, *Achieving National Board Certification for School Library Media Specialists: A Study Guide* (Chicago: American Library Association, 2005).

8
TAKING CHARGE

Most school librarians spend their entire career in a school library, often in the one they took over when they first entered the profession. Because of tenure and other factors, it is in the nature of education for people to remain in one job unless they must move for some reason, the district transfers them to another building, or, as has happened far too often in this economic downturn, they are terminated. However, some of you may decide to advance your career by moving into an administrative position.

The move is not one to take lightly. Even in these times, there are possibly fewer administrators than librarians. Tempting as the possibility of enhanced income might be, you will have little or no contact with students, which has been one of the more rewarding aspects of your job. Before deciding on the move, you need to weigh what you will gain against what you might lose.

BECOMING AN ADMINISTRATOR

No one is going to hand you an administrative job. You will have to actively seek it. If you are fortunate, your district has a supervisor of school libraries or possibly someone who oversees the library program in addition to other hard-to-classify departments such as technology, guidance, or perhaps the nurses. Should you be interested in assuming this position on the departure of the person now in charge, you need to let your interest be known.

More commonly, you will have to look outside your district for opportunities. Large districts are more likely to have supervisors, but it will take research to determine which ones have potential openings. The larger the district, the greater the chance of the school library department having a number of staff members who report to the supervisor. Starting at that level gives you an understanding of what is required when being a part of the district management.

Since these supervisory positions are relatively rare, you might consider becoming a principal instead. Once again, your best chance of doing so is within your own district. The administrators know you and your reputation for leading and getting things done. Have a discussion with a principal with whom you have a strong working relationship. He or she will be aware of potential openings and can help guide you through the process of bringing your name forward.

As with librarianship, you will have preferences for grade level. Do you want to be in an elementary, middle, or high school? Most likely you want the level with which you are most familiar. In a secondary school you would start as an assistant or vice-principal, giving you more of an opportunity to grow into the position of higher responsibility. On the hand, there are more elementary principals, and those at that level often choose to move up to the high school level when an opening occurs. So while you would select one situation over another given the option, the reality is you will seize what is available.

Recognize that there are several downsides to being an administrator besides the ones already mentioned. Paperwork can be overwhelming, as you must document the education process for the state and federal government. Tenure is disappearing in many locations, so you can lose your job at any time. Your expected workday is much longer, and with budget cuts, administrators are doing more work than ever, and summer vacation is limited to four weeks or less.

However, there are good reasons to consider becoming an administrator. You have a greater impact on how teaching and learning occur. If you enjoy the management aspect of being a leader, you will have regular opportunities to grow this aspect of your professional life. Best of all, you can be a champion for the library program.

Taking Charge

1. What would be your ideal first administrative position?
2. What can you do to get this job?
3. What are three good reasons you would want to be an administrator?
4. What are three good reasons for *not* seeking an administrative position?

GOING BACK TO SCHOOL

Once you decide to pursue a path towards administration, you must plan for more schooling. Find out what the requirements are in your state for whatever is the equivalent of supervisory certification and what else is needed to obtain licensing as a principal. Strongly consider a master's degree in education or, even better, an EdD.

Look into the possibility of getting an MBA. With the increasing pressure for schools to operate in a businesslike manner, having an MBA can make you a more attractive candidate for an administrative position. The degree also allows you to become a business administrator or whatever equivalent title is used in a district. Adding this possibility increases your chances for employment.

Next, determine where you will go to acquire the degree. With a busy schedule, you may want to look at an online program. Research the ratings of the schools you are considering. You want to attend the one with the best program. Check the requirements both for being accepted into the program as well as for graduation. If you took the GRE more than five years ago, you may have to retake it. For letters of recommendation, seek those who know of your academic and teaching skills, since they should address your ability to do advanced research. Read the online information the schools provide very carefully. It will guide you in preparing your application, especially in what they expect from your written statement or essay.

If you select a university within your state, you will not have a problem with being certified upon graduation. However, carefully compare courses if you choose to go further afield to be sure the school offers the coursework your state requires for licensure. Since you are unlikely to go full-time, be prepared to spend several years in pursuit of your goal, particularly if you are seeking a doctorate. Many districts will reimburse you for a specified amount per semester if your courses are related to your job and you receive a grade of B or better. You might find that at least some of these do fall within those guidelines which will help with the cost.

Much financial help for graduate work at a local university comes in the form of graduate and teaching assistantships. However, as you have a full-time job in addition to taking courses and dealing with the rest of your life, you will probably find this is not an option. The availability of scholarships varies with institutions. If you need assistance in order to pursue a degree, check the schools you are considering as your choice might rest on what is offered.

While working towards your degree, at some point, you should let your administrators know what you are doing. Besides alerting them to your interest in moving into a managerial position, you can let them know you are open to taking on tasks that will increase your knowledge and skills as a future administrator. What you do can become a topic for a paper or even develop into the subject for your dissertation.

> **A Different Degree**
> 1. Which degree would you seek? Why?
> 2. Which would work better for you, an online, on campus, or blended program?
> 3. Whom would you ask for a recommendation?
> 4. With which administrator would you discuss your plans?

REBUILDING YOUR RESUME

With a degree in hand or when your graduation is in the near future, it is time to actively seek that administrative position. Once again you will be sending out your resume; however, the one you prepared for finding a job as a school librarian will no longer work. You need to re-craft it so you are seen as a strong candidate for this stage of your career plan.

Your *Profile* or *Summary* should reflect your abilities as a leader and project manager. Stress your success in developing a collaborative environment and the results it produced. Of course, communication skills, both oral and written, are important to highlight.

Experience is next, but do not lead off with your school librarian positions. Use *Projects and Committees* as a subhead. This allows you to focus on your credentials as a successful leader. If you headed or chaired any of these, you want to identify your role, then spotlight the achievements of the committee and the outcome or benefits of the projects. What you did as a librarian follows, but tweak what you did to bring the managerial aspects to the forefront.

Follow that section with *Presentations/Workshop* and if you have written anything, include *Publications* as well. Identify the conference and location. Any national appearances should come first, then state, and local presentations. If you displayed at a poster session at a conference, put that here. Education conferences carry greater weight than librarian ones, but all show your work is regarded highly enough to be selected to share with others and that you have the ability to present your ideas to a large group.

Look for opportunities to be published. You need not write a book. At this point, you do not have the time for that, but you can do articles for the various educational journals. Many have themes for each issue and publish these in advance, giving you the opportunity to choose a topic that fits with your experience. If you cannot find this information, contact the editor, preferably of a journal you know and use, suggest a possible article, and see if there is any interest. Do not expect much if any compensation. You are not doing it for that purpose; being published further enhances your professional reputation and makes you a better candidate.

Education comes next, starting with your shiny new degree. If it has not been awarded by the time you send out your resume, specify the date you expect it will be conferred. Add any *Honors and Awards* you have received. *Professional Memberships* completes the resume. Besides proofreading the resume yourself for spelling and grammatical errors, have someone you trust, preferably an administrator, go over it not only to make any corrections you might have missed but also to evaluate it as to how well you promoted yourself as an exceptional candidate for an administrative position.

Resume Redux

1. Which committees and projects have you served on that show your managerial skill?
2. On what topics do you think you could write an article?
3. Which journal(s) would be interested in publishing it?

PREPARING TO BE A FIRST-TIME MANAGER

Now that you are an administrator, you might be tempted to exercise your new power, but do not forget the leadership lessons you learned along the way. Power can be seen as the ability to have someone do or behave in the way you desire. You have been doing that without having any official authority, and you can continue to affect the behavior of others without leaning on the power of your title.

Several business websites[1] discuss the five types of power proposed by French and Raven,[2] and it is wise to know these and recognize which ones are most effective. The five are: Coercive, Reward, Legitimate, Expert, and Referent. The first three are based on your position, while the remaining two are personal and what you have been employing all along.

Coercive power is the ability to punish. In the business world, it translates into firing or demoting someone. In education, it can be the schedule a teacher gets, a transfer, or even the students assigned to a class. It is the iron fist of someone exerting power over another. If people fear you and the repercussions you can visit on them for not adhering to your dictates, they will do what you demand. However, the oppressive climate you create will negate much of your achievements. Heads of large city school systems have garnered headlines for their "bold" actions, but behind the public story is a climate of resentment, low morale, and teachers who leave as soon as they can find employment elsewhere. If you use coercive power, you are not likely to have any one watching your back, and the staff will cheer when you fail.

Reward power is the opposite of coercive, and while it would seem at first glance to be more effective, it still has limitations. As an administrator you cannot give someone more money but you can give them the best "duty" for their assigned period, or a great schedule. The problem is that these people are then seen as the "teacher's pet." Inadvertently you may create resentment, and there will be those who do not want to help you for fear of being tagged as one of your minions.

Legitimate power is that which comes from your position. In essence it describes what you are expected to do as part of your job description. It is legitimate power that is often confused with leadership since one who holds certain titles, such as principal, is expected to be a leader, although as you have seen that is not always the case.

Expert power is what you have wielded in the past to be seen as a leader. When you led or served on a committee people listened to you when research, twenty-first-century skills, and inquiry-based learning were up for discussion. Expert power is a very positive tool because your advice is sought by faculty and administrative colleagues. Your ideas in these areas are likely to move forward more easily because colleagues accept that you know what you are talking about, although you will still have to deal with other issues such as budget, possible personality clashes, and jockeying for position among other administrators.

Referent power is the strongest of all. It is the degree of charisma you possess. Consider it as "star quality." You have been drawing on this as well in developing collaborative partnerships. When people like you, they want to work with you and be a part of whatever you are doing. The greater your referent power, the fewer obstacles you will face. You cannot use it manipulatively, for that will be perceived. It must come from a genuine interest in others, enthusiasm, and skills in minimizing conflicts and confrontations.

In essence, as a manager you want to lead from a place of "power with" rather than the coercive or reward stance of "power over." Show your passion for what you are doing and use it to inspire others rather than compel them to do what you say. Focus on how you can make things work rather than proving you are right.

Avoid arrogance and complacency. These have toppled high-profile CEOs and can have severe consequences for your tenure as an administrator. When you are too certain that you know how to do something or are very sure you are the only one who knows the best way to get a project accomplished, you radiate arrogance. While it might seem at first that you are bulldozing your way to success, there will be too many colleagues and subordinates who will be rooting for your downfall.

When things are going well, it is very easy to become complacent. In his book *Good to Great: Why Some Companies Make the Leap . . . and Others Don't,* Jim Collins opens by saying "Good is the enemy of great."[3] The idea is that too many corporations, institutions, and people inadvertently settle for being good without contemplating what is necessary to become great. When they do so, they accept the status quo and therein lies the path to decline. It is far better to embrace evidenced-based practice which is a process for continuous improvement. You should be familiar with it through Dr. Ross Todd's work on the topic as it applies to school librarianship.[4] Encourage others to use the process as a means of always looking for ways to improve the practice of education.

Most important for any administrator is to celebrate accomplishments of the team. Do not wait until a project is complete. Celebrating achievement should be a regular part of what you do. To avoid appearing as a constant cheerleader, focus on specifics and keep the size of the "celebration" consistent with what has been attained.

Managing Power

1. Where have you seen the negative effects of coercive and reward power?
2. Besides what has been mentioned, what are other areas of your expertise?
3. How have you used "power with" and how has it worked?

LEADING BY LEARNING

As a librarian you are a lifelong learner. This should not change when you assume new responsibilities. Just as your coursework in library school did not fully prepare you, neither will the management and education leadership classes you took ready you for the reality of administrative life. You have observed principals and supervisors in action and used them as good and bad role models, but you have not been privy to the inner workings of district administration or to what must be dealt with on a daily basis.

Once again, you will be expected to hit the ground running. Chances are you will make mistakes. You did so when you first became a librarian. Mistakes are part of the price paid for getting things done. However, you can minimize these by a combination of getting a mentor and honing your active listening skills.

One of the first questions to ask of your mentor is how he or she avoids drowning in the details. You want a method for organizing the workflow that does not overwhelm you but still has you completing the required tasks. Fortunately, you have had some experience with that as a librarian, but you will be surprised at how much paperwork and "showing up" at various events and meetings are an integral part of your day.

If you do not have an acceptable mentor, you will need to develop your own strategy. Start by looking at the district's vision and goals. Note where the superintendent places his or her emphasis, and then craft a mission statement for your job. You need not share this, but it will keep you focused most of the time and get you back on track after unanticipated interruptions.

Listening is key. At meetings, tune into who among the administrators is respected and who is discounted. Are you sensing any cliques or alliances? Are they positive or negative? You want to be cautious about aligning with any group or person until you have a good sense of where they stand.

You also want to listen to teachers and other staff members. The more you actively pay attention to them, the more ownership you will bring to any project, and the more support you will get. Acknowledge the expertise of others. People like real compliments and produce more when their contributions are valued.

Harriette Thurber Rasmussen in an article for *ASCD Express* on "Leadership as Conversation" details how to hold conversations when change is being instituted. She explains the importance of using data to make situations personal and emotional to build urgency. You also must clearly envision what will be needed to reach the desired outcomes, building "collective understanding." Finally, you must be able to look at the data to see to what degree you have achieved the desired goal. Throughout, it is your job to "move people to experiences they would otherwise decline . . . and [bring] about a culture that holds innovation and risk-taking in high esteem."[5]

> ### Ongoing Learning
> 1. What have you learned from a mistake that you made?
> 2. How have you encouraged participant ownership of a project you led?
> 3. Why do you think it is important to make a goal personal?

RISK TAKING

James Bryant Conant, a former president of Harvard University, said, "Behold the turtle. He makes progress only when he sticks his neck out." Those in a position of leadership will do well to remember that. Collaborative decision-making can only go so far. You do not lead by consensus. While you have meaningful conversations to get the broadest input and build ownership, at some point a decision must be made, and it should not be based on a vote.

One of the qualities of leadership that has not been discussed so far is the willingness to take risks. If "good is the enemy of great," you will need to always be looking for ways to do things better, to move into uncharted waters. The fear of taking a risk is one of the greatest failures of leadership whether in education, business, or politics.

Two opposing adages need to be embraced and understood. While it is true that "he who hesitates is lost," it is equally true that "fools rush in where angels fear to tread." Do not attempt to make a change just for the sake of change. You need to have a valid basis for moving in a new direction. Going against a path outlined by upper management is fraught with danger and should only be pursued when you have developed confidence and the reputation for achieving successful results.

A great paralyzer of decision makers is wondering whether they have sufficient information to go ahead. Often this becomes the excuse for not doing anything. In an article by Oren Harari published in the December 1996 issue of *Management Review entitled* "Quotations from Chairman Powell: A Leadership Primer," he lists Colin Powell's lessons, the fifteenth of which is:

> Part I: "Use the formula P = 40 to 70, in which P stands for the probability of success and the numbers indicate the percentage of information acquired."
> Part II: "Once the information is in the 40 to 70 range, go with your gut."[6]

While 40 percent is probably too low a number in the education world for you to base whether or not to go with a risk, accept the underlying concept that you will never have 100 percent of the possible information. As Powell goes on to say, "Procrastination in the name of reducing risk actually increases risk."[7]

So how can you take risks without being reckless? What can you do to maximize the likelihood for success? Obviously, gather information. Find out if your idea has been tried elsewhere and with what results. Were any mistakes made that, given what they learned along the way, could be avoided? Look for new ideas. Search outside the library and education professions. Become aware of trends, concepts, and practices in business and technology. Keep an eye on the political scene at the state and national levels. Research the direction in which politicians seem to be heading so you can anticipate positive and negative results and lead the way to being prepared for them.

Next, work with a team to further explore the possibility of implementing your idea. Set a date by when a decision will be made. Decide what needs to be known in order to determine whether or not to go ahead with the project. Have assignments for team members and let them know by when they must report their findings.

Once you have approval to go ahead with the plan, have your team work out the best way to launch it. Members should identify those likely to be early adopters and what approach will potentially get them on board. Who will resist? Why? What, if anything, can be done to minimize their reactions?

You might want to look at the "pencil metaphor" (http://positivedv8r.files.wordpress.com/2010/10/pencil-metaphor.png) to remember that in any organization you will always have the groups the metaphor characterizes. Although the focus in the illustration is on technology integration, recognize that these people are a constant and respond this way to whatever change is proposed. Being familiar with them allows you to anticipate their reactions and plan how you will respond.

While a mark of a good leader is the willingness to take risks, a certain amount of caution is wise. Being foolhardy will not gain you respect. If you take a major risk and fail, you jeopardize your new position. You do not test the depth of unknown waters with both feet. Start small and learn from each attempt. Slowly you will build both experience and reputation which will give you credibility when you are ready to propose a large change.

For example, if you think that a mentorship program would help new teachers, start with one department. Be sure key players are interested and willing. Have mentor and mentee keep track of what works and what does not. Avoid micromanaging. Limit your check-ins to not more than once a month. At the end of the year, assess this pilot program to see if it is worthy of expansion. By limiting the scope of the project initially, you gather a wealth of information that will minimize the risk should you decide to recommend it as a school- or district-wide program.

One final word about risk—you will fail at times. That is why it is a risk. However, failing is not a bad thing if you learn from it. Retreating to nurse your wounds and fearing to take another chance in the future is the true failure. Analyze what went wrong. What could or should you have done differently? How will this help you be more successful the next time?

Risk Management

1. Why should administrators and leaders be willing to take risks?
2. What risks have you taken in your life and/or career?
3. Did you have all the information when you decided to take it? How did it turn out?
4. Looking at the "Pencil Metaphor," to which group do *you* belong?
5. What have you learned from a failure?

MANAGING AN INTERVIEW

Now that you are an administrator, you will be interviewing applicants for positions in your school district. Hiring the wrong candidate is costly on many levels. If you need to replace that person, you will lose time and possibly money in re-advertising the slot. Even more significant is the cost to students and staff who have had to deal with someone who was not suitable.

To reduce the possibility of making the wrong choice, you need to prepare in advance as much as you did when you were interviewing to obtain a job. Prepare a list of questions that you will ask *every* candidate. While you will add to it based on an individual's resume and responses, having answers from everyone to the same questions gives you an across-the-board basis for comparison.

The standard interview questions discussed in chapter 2 will be useful to you as you now sit on the other side of the desk, but you might want to reach deeper. Bob Herbold, former chief operating officer at Microsoft Corporation, suggests asking candidates what person taught them valuable lessons about life when they were young. He follows it by inquiring what those lessons were and how these have become guiding principles. Herbold contends that the responses let you know the individual's motivations and their drive for success.[8]

Read over the resumes and cover letters with care. Does anything jump out at you? How many years have the candidates been in this field? How long have they remained in previous positions? Are there any red flags? What do they regard as their strengths and accomplishments? Will these be a good fit for the opening? Does it seem as though they took time and paid attention to their resumes and cover letters?

Be mindful of the verbal and nonverbal messages interviewees send. A certain amount of nervousness is normal, but notice whether they reflect before responding. While a quick mind is a good attribute, you want prospective hires to exhibit thoughtfulness, not just go with the first answer that comes into their heads. How focused are their responses? Do they need to backtrack because they left something out? Are they rambling and including extraneous details?

Listen to their voices. Some people have a way of speaking that implies judgment of others. You might sense a suppressed level of anger. Do they appear unsure, confident, or cocky about their knowledge? Have they done their homework about the district and know what contribution they believe they can make? If one of your questions stymies them, do they ask for clarification, try to bluff their way through, or admit to not being ready to respond at this time?

Keep an eye on their hands and body language in general. Are they fidgeting or seem flustered? Are nerves keeping them from being able to really listen to what is being asked? Do they look at the person posing the question? If more than one interviewer is present, do they include everyone when giving their answers? No one is going to be perfect in all aspects, but these will give you clues as who the candidate is as a person and how he or she is likely to behave in stressful situations.

If at all possible, have anyone who will be working with the candidate be present at the interview. While you might not be able to tell if there will be "good chemistry," you are likely to discover if the personalities might clash. Discuss reactions from these participants as soon as the interviewee leaves. Trust your intuition as to whether the interviewee will be a good fit for the position and the school. You are undoubtedly picking up signals you were not aware that you noticed.

Hire Standards

1. Which questions from your own interview would you definitely want to include when looking to hire someone?
2. How would you answer Bob Herbold's interview question that should always be asked?
3. What skills have you acquired that will help you successfully interview a candidate?

MANAGING MEETINGS

Although you have managed meetings as you grew in your job, you will be doing so increasingly often. Those attending may be your equals or subordinates but all, to some extent, will be judging you on how you lead. What you must be able to project is a combination of leadership and management. The distinction is not always understood, but it is important. Leaders lead. They have a big picture view and a personal vision for where things are heading. As noted earlier, they are willing to take risks and make difficult decisions. Managers know how to build a collaborative environment. They are aware of and have an appreciation for the special talents and skills of their colleagues and subordinates and create a climate that inspires them to produce their best.

As a leader you are in charge of the meeting. You set the start and end time. It is up to you to ensure that it begins promptly and finishes when scheduled. This not only demonstrates your organizational skills but also shows you respect the time of others. Have a clear purpose, which should be shared with everyone. In your own mind, know the desired outcomes even if you cannot predict the specifics.

In other words, you must prepare. Develop an agenda and send it out in advance. Include an opening to set the tone and focus the meeting and a conclusion to sum up what was accomplished. Review any actions to be taken, who will be doing them, and when they are to report back. Set the date and time of the next meeting, checking to be sure that it fits everyone's—or almost everyone's—schedule. Be flexible enough to make adjustments to ensure maximum attendance.

Display your management skills by asking for input when you send out the agenda. Call it a draft, identifying when you need to know what others want added so you have time to circulate the final agenda. Be sure you are not doing most of the talking. Let those who suggested items be the ones who bring them to the table. See how they manage the discussion. This gives you an understanding of their leadership ability and allows you time to observe more easily the degree to which everyone is actually participating.

Unless you are trying to assess someone's performance, have people volunteer for any proposed actions rather than making assignments. Encourage partnerships when possible and then keep an eye on how these are working. If you have managed a safe, collaborative climate you will be informed if anyone is having difficulty meeting the deadlines that were set. If you feel the need to inspect the progress being made, be careful not to sound as though you are micromanaging or not trusting those working on the assignment. Instead, say something like, "Let me know how things are going. Ask if you need some help or want an extension."

Little things count. When holding the first meeting of a big project, have folders or ring binders, pads, and pens for everyone. You may end up doing most of your work online using a wiki or putting reports and research in LiveBinders (www.livebinders.com), but many still like hard copy, and giving small stationery items always makes people feel more valued and respected. Food is another "big, little thing." Budgets in many places have eliminated providing lunches, but you can bring in cookies or doughnuts even if you pay for them out of your own pocket and you can usually get beverages.

Meetings of Minds

1. What do you think is an ideal meeting length?
2. How do you want people to feel going into a meeting you are leading? What can you do to create that attitude?
3. How do you want people to feel when they leave the meeting? What do you have to do to ensure that?

BROADENING YOUR PERSPECTIVE

You would think that by now you already have a broad perspective. As a librarian, you dealt with students over the entire grade range of the building. You might have been aware of the curriculum for a variety of subject areas or grade levels. As an administrator you become knowledgeable about the district as a whole. Yet this is still not enough.

In becoming a leader and advancing your career (and your program) when you were in the library, you joined your state and national organizations, becoming an active, participating member. You attended conferences and served on committees either in person or virtually and developed an extensive personal learning network (PLN). You must do the same in your new position.

Join the Association for Supervision and Curriculum Development (ASCD), www.ascd.org. Its journal and publications are among the best in education. Also become a member of whatever association serves your position, such as the Association for Secondary School Principals (even if you are a vice-principal). Go to their conferences and get to know the leaders and shakers in the field. When you are ready, and do not wait too long, propose a program for a conference. Getting your name out there is important, bringing you to the attention of the leadership of these organizations.

If you have become the head of the technology department you almost certainly are a member of the International Society for Technology Education (ISTE), www.iste.org. You also should be a member of the Association for Educational Communications and Technology (AECT), www.aect.org. The former has a special interest group for librarians and technology directors and the latter has divisions for them. In your new position you can be of invaluable service to the school library program.

Whatever national or state organization you join, volunteer to serve on a committee. To the extent that it is possible, seek out one that connects with something you are doing in your district. You will bring more context and understanding to both areas this way.

Once you have become familiar with the operations of the association, become a candidate for an office. While this entails extra work, the rewards

---

The View from (Near) the Top

1. Whom will you seek to include in your PLN?
2. To which organizations do you belong that will serve you in your new position?
3. Which ones will you need to join?
4. What committees do they have that would be of interest to you?

more than outweigh the additional time you will be committing. Connecting with colleagues from different districts in your state—or across the nation—will enhance your awareness of issues of common concern, how they are being handled in other places, and what you should bring back to your district.

Your PLN will grow and evolve as you take on larger roles. Each time you gain access to a richer source of information and support. At some point in the future you might decide to move on to another district or a new level of management. The relations you have made through these associations will be a resource from which you can draw.

CREATING A POSITIVE WORK ENVIRONMENT

In developing the leadership ability that brought you to this level, you have mastered many of the skills necessary for creating an environment in which people become participatory members, eager to contribute to the educational community. In settling into your new position, do not lose sight of the importance of ensuring that you continue to maintain and expand those positive attitudes. Be conscious of your behaviors and attitudes towards subordinates as much as you are aware of your interactions with superiors.

Your emotional intelligence is a key factor. Some of the people with whom you have worked collegially in the past may be uncertain as to whether you will continue to be the same person in your new position. Keeping up these relationships and showing you continue to care about them will go far in reassuring those who are wondering. If you are working in the same district, you will be helped by having connections with colleagues who have come to trust you. You know procedures and are not likely to inadvertently step on someone's toes or alienate a necessary ally.

Starting in a new district is more challenging. Focus on empathy, developing a participatory culture, and being as transparent as possible. These are the foundations of a positive work environment. Move carefully at first and build relationships. Your active listening skills will help you quickly identify the culture and the informal power structure that underlies the district. Knowing these, you can move ahead, confident that the climate you create will not only serve to improve the educational quality of the district but will ensure that your colleagues will help you avoid any pitfalls.

It's Good to Work Here
1. Would you prefer to have an administrative position in your current district or to start it somewhere else? Why?
2. What are three things you can do to create a positive work environment?

KEY IDEAS

- Attaining an administrative position requires you to actively seek out what is available.
- Make your interest known if you want an administrative position in your current district.
- Weigh the pros and cons of becoming an administrator.
- Consider getting an EdD or an MBA when planning for this career move.
- Choose your graduate school with care, researching requirements and ratings.
- Revise your resume to reflect your administrative and leadership skills.
- Look for opportunities to be published in recognized educational journals.
- Know the five types of power and focus on the positive ones.
- Celebrate the achievements of those on your team.
- Get a mentor to guide you in your new position.
- Acknowledge and seek out the expertise of others.
- Know how and be willing to take risks.
- Prepare a set of questions which you will pose to all potential hires for a given position.
- Read resumes in advance with an eye to red flags as well as clues to the candidates' mental habits.
- Be aware of candidates' body language and voice cues.
- Have those who will work with the new hire present at the interview, if possible.
- Trust your instincts on candidates.
- Understand the difference between leading and managing and know when to do each.
- Prepare an agenda in advance of meetings and circulate it to those attending.
- Start and end meetings on time.
- Show respect to those participating in the meetings.
- Join appropriate national and state administrator associations and become an active member.
- Develop a PLN.
- Employ your emotional intelligence to create a positive work environment.

NOTES

1. "Mind Tool: French and Raven's Five Forms of Power," www.mindtools.com/pages/article/newLDR_56.htm.
2. John R. P. French, Jr., and Bertram Raven, "The Bases of Social Power," in *Group Dynamics*, ed. D. Cartwright and A. Zander (New York: Harper and Row, 1960), 607–23.
3. Jim Collins, *Good to Great: Why Some Companies Make the Leap . . . and Others Don't*. (New York: HarperBusiness, 2001), 1.
4. Ross Todd, "The Evidence-Based Manifesto for School Librarians," *School Library Journal*, April 1, 2008, www.schoollibraryjournal.com/article/CA6545434.html.
5. Harriette Thurber Rasmussen, "Leadership as Conversation," *ASCD Express* 7, no. 6 (December 22, 2011), www.ascd.org/ascd-express/v017/706-rasmussen.aspx?utm_source=ascdexpress&utm_medium=email&utm_campaign=express706.
6. Oren Harari, "Quotations from Chairman Powell: A Leadership Primer," http://govleaders.org/powell2.htm.
7. Ibid.
8. "A Critical Interview Question You Should Always Ask," www.thoughtleadersllc.com/2011/12/a-revealing-interview-question.

9
MOVING ON

Rarely does a career go completely as planned. Life events interfere. Administrations change and what once was a wonderful situation becomes filled with stress. A partner's job offer involves moving to another location. Certainly, you have seen and possibly experienced the impact of an economic downturn. Even if all has gone well, you will arrive at the point when you start thinking about retirement.

Whether you make the decision to leave or it is forced, you still want to have a direction in which to go. You can start a new and enriching chapter in your life, bringing you unexpected rewards. Research, analysis, evaluation, and planning—tools you have developed over time—will help you to successfully manage this next stage of your life.

WHEN TO LEAVE AND HOW TO DO IT

Although those in education usually do not leave a position voluntarily unless they are transferring to another school in the district, moving to another more distant location, or taking on an administrative job, there are good reasons to resign. Job situations can change and when they do, your attitude changes with it. Hoping things will get better is not a positive way of dealing with new circumstances.

In many places, the "great recession" has affected what you are expected to do and not for the better. Librarians who had only one school now have two or more. Middle and high schools that had two librarians are now down to one. Support staff have all but disappeared in countless locations. Some of you are now expected to teach one or more non-library classes. What can you do?

Most will tell you that having a job is what is important and you need to stay put. Finding another job is extremely difficult in this climate, so that advice has much merit. Before thinking about resigning, look for ways to improve the situation you are in. Recognize you cannot do everything you did before. Focus on your mission statement to identify your core purpose and then analyze what in your current day contributes to it and what diminishes it. Develop priorities for what you most want to accomplish and what you think needs to be eliminated. Discuss this with your administrators to get approval.

While you can expect modifications, you may not get much of what you want. What you do next depends on how stressed you become with what you are now doing and what you can do about that. Stress affects how you interact with students, teachers, your family—basically everyone in your life. When you lose the joy in going to work, everyone around you suffers and so do you.

Stress also has an effect on the immune system and can harm you physically. Is the job worth that? The answer is a personal one, but you need to be honest with yourself. If you must stay, then recognize why you have made that choice. What is the "higher good" for which you are, at least for now, sacrificing your well-being? When you know what is at stake, it is easier to face each day.

Even when the economy is not in disarray, your job situation can change. A new administrator is hired who has little understanding or appreciation for the school library program. You do your best, using all the tools previously discussed, to promote what you do but nothing seems to change his or her preconceived ideas. You could wait it out and hope that person will move on, but that is not a proactive way to be.

Another reason for considering leaving a position is when your school seems to be locked in the past. Technology changes come slowly and the culture is resistant to it. The longer you stay the more your skills deteriorate and the less opportunity you have to build your own knowledge base.

Whatever the reason, when you decide it is time to leave you must plan carefully and behave professionally. In addition to checking the job listings to see what is available, draw on the network you have established. Your librarian colleagues are obvious sources, although you want to be sure they will be discreet. If you have dealings with publishers' representatives who visit you in person, let them know as well. They cover the territory and speak with librarians, frequently knowing of upcoming openings before these are announced.

Once you have identified one or more possibilities, research the district, and update your resume. If you are asked to come for an interview, be prepared to explain why you are seeking a new position. Never say anything negative about your current school, the administration, or the teachers. Put the focus on your commitment to students and the benefits of an active school library program. Explain that hard decisions or altered directions (depending on whether the issue is financial or administrative changes) have made it difficult for you to deliver the program you feel students and teachers deserve and need.

Finding a new job will take time. Openings are scarce in the current climate, but you still do not want to take the first one that comes along unless you know it will be an improvement. There is no sense in jumping out of the frying pan to go into the fire. Once you do discover the right fit, be professional about leaving. Present your resignation letter to your administrator in person. State your reasons for leaving in the same terms that you used in the interview. Avoid any negatives. You never know when your career paths will cross again.

Time to Go?

1. What would make you want to leave your job voluntarily?
2. What would be good reasons for staying even if the situation deteriorated?
3. How could you minimize the stress from a job that has affected your ability to deliver a library program that meets twenty-first-century needs?

RELOCATING

As soon as your partner takes a job in another state, start the process to find a new position. Become familiar with and preferably join the state's school library association. See if their website lists openings. Announce your upcoming move on their electronic discussion list and ask if anyone is aware of available jobs.

Find out if your certification is transferable. Many times you need to take one or more courses in order to be able to be a librarian in another state. Locate the schools that offer these and be prepared to register as soon as possible.

Use a map of the state to identify districts within a reasonable commute of your new home. Go to their websites and get a feel for their approach to education and the importance they place on the school library program. If at all possible, visit some of the librarians and discuss with them what possibilities they see for openings in the near future.

Do they hire substitutes for the school librarians? If so, what do you have to do to get on the list? In many districts that is the best avenue to being offered a job. Consider being a substitute for classroom teachers as well since you will be called more often. This not only gives you a better income stream but also keeps you on the administrators' radar. On the flip side, you get to know the schools and the districts much better and can focus your efforts on the more desirable locations.

Networking is increasingly one of the best ways to find a job. If you belong to AASL, ISTE, or AECT, use their electronic discussion lists or special interest groups to find people in the state to which you are relocating. Once you have identified one or more, contact them for information asking about any openings.

You can also use LinkedIn (www.linkedin.com), which has become the top social networking site for finding jobs. Develop a complete profile, highlighting your special skills. Ask for "recommendations" which are then posted on your page. Make connections with people in the school library field and then send a message stating that you are looking for a position and why. The more people who know you are involved in a job search, the more likely that someone will know of an opening and contact you.

While LinkedIn is very well known in the business world, you may not get much in the way of response as school librarians are still in the early stage of discovering how best to use it. Try your other social networks to increase your chances of making contact with people who can help you. Post it on your status on Facebook and tweet about it every other week. You do not want to annoy your friends, but do let them know how your job search is progressing. Keep looking for new avenues to increase your networking. Eventually someone will contact you.

Making a Move

1. How many school librarians do you know who live in other states?
2. Do you belong to Facebook? Do you post fairly often?
3. Are you on LinkedIn? When did you last update your profile?

GETTING BACK TO WORK

What can you do when you are trying to get back into the job market after having been away from it for one or more years? Whether you have been unemployed by choice and now want to return to work or have been one of the many who were laid off during the economic crisis, finding a position is a daunting challenge. Losing your job is a frightening experience and can be paralyzing, at least in the short term. Trying to get back into work is often an uphill struggle made worse by current conditions.

Planning and networking will help move you from fear and possible loss of self-esteem into a more positive frame of mind and potentially lead to your next job. Use those ideas discussed in the section on relocating that are applicable to your situation, but do not just wait for something to turn up. While hunting for a position, be proactive. Those who have been out of work for a long time are likely not to have the latest technology skills. If you are recently unemployed, you do not want to allow your knowledge base to deteriorate.

Consider taking a course related to librarianship. You might not want to add an expense when you do not have a job, but think of it as an investment in your career. Also you will be adding to your contacts. Your professor might know of openings, or your fellow students can be a source of information. In the meantime, you are expanding your knowledge base.

Webinars are another means of increasing your knowledge and are far cheaper than a college class. AASL regularly offers its e-Academy, a series of four-week online courses. They are twelve hours each and participants receive a certificate after completing a culminating project. Search "e-Academy" at the AASL website (www.ala.org/aasl) to learn what is currently available.

Seek opportunities to volunteer in a library. School libraries are the best choice and will look good on your resume. Do not volunteer to replace a librarian whose job was eliminated. You would only compound the problem and lead the administration to believe that there is no need to ever rehire a certificated person. However, you can help where support staff has been reduced or never existed. Working with the librarian, you can keep up (or learn what you have missed over the years) with the technology resources that are being integrated into the library and school programs. Because you do not have the same responsibilities, you have time to explore databases in depth and experiment with new tools, developing your proficiency. You also have the opportunity to observe how a colleague manages a program and see what you would or would not want to emulate.

Volunteering also gives you an opportunity to work at different grade levels. You may have been a high school librarian and now are in an elementary school. Discovering the development that occurs over the years will be helpful when you do get a job. If the reverse is true, you learn what skills younger students need to develop to be successful when they reach secondary school. Just as with substitute teaching, your presence in the building and becoming known to teachers and administrators can position you for being offered a job when an opening does occur.

Consider volunteering in a public or even academic library. The pace and focus are different but you will still be honing your skills. In public libraries you can continue to work with students who are at the same age range as in your former school library. The breadth of resources for research in academic libraries will expand your understanding of what students should know before entering college. You may enjoy your new situation so much that you will choose to seek employment there rather than in a school system.

While you are busy volunteering, stay in contact with your professional network. Include the staff with whom you are now working, but keep up with those still in the field. You want to find out about any opening as soon as it occurs. Staying active and continuing to learn will make you more secure about what you will bring to your next position.

Take stock of skills you have that might be marketable. Those of you recently out of work who are adept at the latest technology might want to look at the possibility of doing "content creation" as suggested in a *Library Journal* article.[1] Look for important blogs and other online information sources that might pay you for what you can do. Even if you only can find non-paying positions, you will be keeping your resume current and perhaps find new networking possibilities.

Working to Get Back to Work

1. Check local and online graduate school offerings. What course(s) would expand your skills and get you excited and motivated?
2. Which of the AASL e-Academy courses appeals to you?
3. Would you rather volunteer in a public or a school library? What would be the lure of each?
4. Create a list of your professional network contacts and keep in touch with them. Maintaining the relationship makes it easy to reach out when one of you needs assistance.
5. What are your marketable skills?

TEACHING AT GRADUATE SCHOOL

Whether you are working full-time or are seeking employment, becoming an adjunct professor (or lecturer) is a great part-time job. Community colleges are bursting at the seams with students who are using it as a cheaper way to fund a four-year college education and with out-of-work professionals seeking to hone old or develop new skills. You can look far afield for possible openings since there are now so many online programs.

Teaching at the graduate level has its own rewards as, unlike elementary or high school students, these students are eager to hear what you have to offer. They have sought out the course and program and are highly motivated. It can be a heady experience to be regarded as a "font of wisdom." Aside from the ego boost, you deepen your own understanding of the course content. Teaching is always the best way to learn.

Once you are hired, you must prepare your course. It is easiest if you have an existing syllabus from which to work, but you may have to create one. Contact the department chair to obtain some samples you can use as a template, and then determine what topics will be covered and how you will assess students' understanding of the material. If it has been a while since you were in graduate school yourself, do not fall back on teaching the way you were taught. Collaboration and products other than research papers are as much a presence here as they are in elementary and secondary schools.

Online teaching has special challenges. You will need to become skilled at whatever software is being used. If the university is not too distant from where you live, you can generally get on-site, hands-on training from the information technology (IT) department. When the school is remote, you will have to rely on online tutorials that are provided. You can always e-mail, text, or talk with the IT people if and when you are confused about something.

Some of you may discover you prefer teaching at this level and seek to make it a full-time career. Although not always necessary, you will have a better chance at advancement within the academic structure with a doctoral degree. If you are considering this alternative, find one or two colleagues who have made the move and talk to them about the positives and negatives and why they chose to teach graduate school. One of them may become a mentor.

Higher Education

1. What graduate course(s) do you think you are qualified to teach?
2. Would you rather teach online, face-to-face, or a hybrid course?

ACADEMIC AND PUBLIC LIBRARIANSHIP

If you would rather remain in a library setting, becoming an academic or public librarian offers a satisfying career change for school librarians. Unlike teaching at the graduate level, you do not have the online option, so your location may make finding a position difficult. If you live relatively near several two- and four-year colleges, you can check their websites for employment opportunities. Visit the schools and speak with the librarians who might give you suggestions or alert you to possible upcoming openings.

Academic librarianship has changed over the years so you would still have opportunities to teach classes as well as the more expected working one-on-one with students. As you might expect, they are intimidated by the extensive databases which they are expected to use in their research. You will need to learn those databases' breadth and depth as well.

Reference questions and research projects are more sophisticated than those of high school students, but the college freshmen are not that different from the high school seniors whom you know well. Your ability to relate to them will be a big help in acclimating them as well as you. Despite being in college, they bring with them the "research strategies" they employed in high school. As you might expect, their first instincts are to search on YouTube, Google, and *Wikipedia*. If their librarian had not trained them well, you will be the one to teach them to refine their search terms, use *Wikipedia* discerningly, and, of course, discover the databases related to their topics.

In making the change to academic librarianship you should be prepared for the need to become familiar with the collection and the use of the Library of Congress Classification System and Subject Headings, as well as the sheer size of the library. However, you may overlook some of the more rewarding benefits. Most school librarians work alone, but college libraries, even smaller ones, have a staff of several librarians and various types of clerical assistance. You have colleagues who can help you learn your way around your new situation, unlike in school systems where you must figure out most procedures on your own. The support from the IT department is also a welcome change from what many of you experience in your current situations.

Public librarianship also affords you more colleagues on a daily basis. Working in the children's or young adult department is an easy transition. While you no longer will be instructing classes, you will be helping students with their assignments and locating the leisure reading they love.

You will also be developing programming to meet the interests of these students. The Young Adult Library Services Association has numerous special weeks and days and its website at www.ala.org/yalsa offers ideas for all of them, from Teen Tech Week and Teen Read Week to National Gaming Day programs. If you work in a children's department, the American Association for Library Services to Children has two initiatives: El día de los niños/El día de los libros (Children's Day/Book Day), or Día, which culminates annually on April 30 and is a daily celebration of children, families, and reading emphasizing advocacy for children's literacy of all linguistic and cultural backgrounds; and Every Child Ready to Read, which helps parents and caregivers develop early literacy skills in children from birth to age five. See www.ala.org/alsc/initiatives for more details.

As with academic librarianship, you will be surrounded by colleagues and staff—unless you are in a small branch. Your days may not be as hectic, but your workweek is usually longer and you can expect to be scheduled for at least one weekend day on a rotating basis. Of course, you will no longer have summer vacations. Four weeks are typical. On the other hand, you have much more flexibility in arranging your time off. Another bonus is that both academic and public librarians are often in a different pension plan from the school systems, giving you another income stream for your retirement. This may be available even if you are part-time.

For those of you who entered school librarianship via the classroom, the public library experience can be a revelation. In schools, the emphasis is on instruction, so often student questions are answered with guidance that sends them back to use their skills to find the information they were seeking. Public libraries put the focus on service, usually offering immediate help. Should you return to school librarianship, you will likely be more conscious of when to provide assistance and when to give support for building skills.

A Library by Another Name
1. What, if anything, do you find appealing about academic librarianship?
2. What do you like most about public librarianship?
3. Which of the two would you prefer?

RETIREMENT

You have had a great career, but you are finally contemplating retiring. Aside from checking with your pension plan and social security, the most important planning you can do is to decide what you will be retiring *to*. If you are just retiring *from*, you will begin the process of rusting away. As the lifelong learner you are, you need to know what you will be doing in retirement.

First of all, continue your membership in your national and state library associations. Did you know that if you have been a member of the ALA for twenty-five continuous years, you have free dues upon retirement? You still need to pay for your division membership, but that is a small amount in comparison. AASL has also started a special interest group for retirees. Here you can maintain or improve your skills, discuss books with your colleagues across the country, get involved in research projects, and even "pay it forward" by mentoring or advising new school librarians.

The opportunities for mentoring and doing other significant work for the profession also occur within your state organization. Many times the president of your association is invited to meetings during the school day. Getting release time from schools is almost impossible, but you can be the president's representative at those meetings. Since they are not working, retirees can also serve on multi-type library committees such as the one for the Library Services and Technology Act, which is organized at the state level, or the Center for the Book. In some states, New Jersey is one, retirees are the major volunteers at the state conference, having their registration fee waived in return for their service.

The earlier suggestions for volunteering in school and public libraries are good possibilities for using your skills and investing your time for a worthy purpose. Those of you who worked part-time will probably enjoy it more now that you have a freer schedule. Keeping this door open is a good idea as life events both financial and personal may cause you to want to return to full-time work.

A school librarian who wanted to give back to her community found several means for doing so. Twice a week, she volunteers at a psychiatric hospital where, without any funds, she set up a library for its clients and is now creating a virtual medical library for the staff. Still using her computer skills, she also works at a local food bank doing data entry of the monthly reports from participating pantries, shelters, and soup kitchens. As if that were not enough, this "retired" librarian volunteers once a month at a shelter, preparing dinner and helping kids with their homework. Believe it or not, she performs other community services on a regular basis.

The quotation marks around the word "retired" allude to a truth for many librarians. They find these years are more filled and more fulfilling than the ones they spent in school libraries. Besides volunteering, you can apply your experience at collection development in a new way by working for a publisher's representative and visiting school and public libraries to show the latest titles. You have the background to explain how these fit within the curriculum and suggest ways of using them collaboratively with teachers. If you keep your territory small, you need only work a few days a week.

Bring your expertise to creating a blog for your colleagues. With more available time, you can seek out new online resources to make research easier and presentations more interesting. You can play with these resources and report on their ease of use. Once you get the word out, busy librarians will seek what you have posted, grateful that someone else has done the digging and evaluating.

Of course, you might delve more deeply into hobbies and other interests. Whether it is gardening, family genealogy, or any other pursuit, you can indulge those passions which had to be placed on a back burner during the years you were working. Nevertheless, you are likely to find that you bring your librarianship with you. Your researching skills and your disposition as a lifelong learner will continue to keep your mind active and your knowledge growing.

> **Not Quite Retired**
> 1. How do you see yourself contributing and participating in your professional associations after retirement?
> 2. Which of the possibilities discussed most appeal to you for your retirement years?
> 3. How will you go about adding these to your life?

KEY IDEAS

- Research, analysis, evaluation, and planning will help you when you are leaving your job.
- When your work situation is negatively changed, you need to determine whether or not to seek another position.
- Do not remain in a poor, stress-filled situation unless you are clear why staying is worth what you are sacrificing.
- If you do decide to resign, use your personal professional network to learn of possible openings and behave professionally.
- When relocating, use your social networks to find openings and get up to speed about the new area to which you are going.
- Taking courses, signing up for webinars, and volunteering at school or public libraries will help you get up to speed if you are returning to the job market after years away and will help you maintain your skills if you are out of work.
- Assess your marketable skills and use them to be involved with activities that will keep your resume from showing a gap in time.
- Teaching at the graduate level, even part-time, can prove to be financially rewarding as well as expanding your own learning and enhancing your resume.
- Working in an academic or public library can be a mentally and emotionally stimulating career shift.
- Continue to contribute and learn by maintaining your membership in your professional association.
- Consider part-time work in related but non-library situations such as becoming a publisher's representative.
- Become a writer of blogs, books, or other outlets to serve the profession or your own interests.
- Follow your passions, but know that once a librarian, always a librarian. You are always a lifetime learner.

NOTE

1. John Farrier, "Digital Content Curation Is Career for Librarians: Backtalk," *Library Journal,* February 1, 2012, http://lj.libraryjournal.com/2012/02/opinion/backtalk/digital-content-curation-is-a-perfect-career-fit-for-librarians-backtalk.

INDEX

A

AASL. *See* American Association for School Librarians (AASL)
academic librarianship, 117–118
Achieving National Board Certification for School Library Media Specialists: A Study Guide (Dickinson), 85
active listening, 64. *See also* listening
   body language and, 40
   collaboration and, 81
   for on the job learning, 38–39
active observation
   body language and, 40
   for on the job learning, 39
administrators. *See also* leaders; leadership
   asking help from, 52–54
   becoming, 93–94
   broadening perspectives and, 106–107
   creating positive work environments and, 107–108
   graduates degrees for becoming, 95
   on the job learning from, 40
   listening and, 100
   managing interviews and, 103–104
   managing meetings and, 104–105
   managing up and, 63–65
   preparation for first-time, 97–99
   resumes for, 96–97
   schooling for, 95–96
advocacy programs
   considerations for developing, 59–60
   for library programs, 58–59
   toolkits for developing, 59

ALA (American Library Association), conferences of, 49–50
ALA JobLIST, as resource for first job, 3
American Association for Library Services to Children, 118
American Association for School Librarians (AASL)
   conferences of, 49
   e-Academy, 49
   "Exploratorium" session, 74
   for professional development, 49
American Library Association (ALA), conferences of, 49–50
arrogance, administrators and, 98
Association for Education Communication and Technology (AECT), 51, 106
Association for Secondary School Principals, 106
Association for Supervision and Curriculum Development (ASCD), 106
   professional development publications, 50
attire, for interviews, 14
author visits, hosting, 54–55

B

Baumbach, Donna J., 76
blog posts, hazards of, 4
book fairs, hosting, 54
brevity, communication and, 68
budgets, preparing, for library programs, 56–58

C

career centers, as resource for writing resumes, 6
certification, obtaining, 84–96

123

charter schools, employment in, 35–36
clarity
    communication and, 68
    leaders and, 80–81
clothing, for interviews, 14
coercive power, 97–98
collaboration
    developing relationships and, 70–71
    emotions and, 83
    listening and, 81
    school librarians and, 70
    understanding emotions and, 83
    units, developing, 70–71
college placement offices, 2
Collins, Jim, 99
committees, gaining experience by being on, 43–44
communication skills
    leaders and, 68–69, 80–81
    oral, 69
    for presentations at conferences, 72–74
community outreach, leadership and, 85–87
complacency, administrators and, 98
Conant, James Bryant, 100
conferences
    of American Library Association, 49–50
    communication skills for presentations at, 72–74
    for professional development, 49–50
conflicts of interest, 89
cover letters, 9–11. *See also* resumes
curriculum-writing committees, 43

D

departures. *See* resignations
Dickinson, Gail, 85
district professional development, 47–48

E

e-Academy (American Association for School Librarians), 49
e-mail, for sending resumes, 6–7
e-mail cover letters, 10
education associations, 50
elementary school library positions, interview questions for, 15
emotional intelligence (EI)
    active listening and, 84
    active observation and, 84
    creating positive work environments and, 107–108
    high, 84
    tuning in, 82–84

emotions
    collaboration and, 83
    managing, 84
    negative, 84
    positive, 84
    reasoning with, 83
empathy, leaders and, 81
employers, researching prospective, 7–9
events, running, 54–56
experience, gaining on the job, 43–44
expert power, 98

F

fillers, speech, 69
Financial Assistance for library and Information Studies (American Library Association), 51
first jobs, resources for searching for, 2–3
first-time managers, preparing for becoming, 97–99
focus groups, 88–89
follow-up calls, 22
fonts, for resumes, 5
formats, for resumes, 5–6
Foundation Center, 52
Foundation Directory Online, 52

G

Good to Great: Why Some Companies Make the Leap . . . and Others Don't (Collins), 99
graduate degrees, becoming an administrator and, 95–96
graduate schools, teaching at, 116–117
grants, for master's degrees, 51–52

H

Harari, Oren, 101
helicopter parents, 35
Herbold, Bob, 103

I

Imagination, Cognitions, and Personality (Salovey and Mayer), 82
in-house professional development, 48
in-person interviews, 17–19. *See also* interviews
International Society for Technology, 106
interview outfits, proper, 14
interview questions
    for elementary school library positions, 15
    practicing for, 14–17
    samples, 16
    for secondary school library positions, 15

INDEX

interviews
    activities after, 21–22
    administrators and managing, 103–104
    in-person, 17–19
    preparing for, 13–17
    sample questions for, 15, 16
    telephone, 19–20

J

jobs, resources for searching first, 2–3
job market, reentering, 114–116
job offers
    multiple, 27–28
    understanding and evaluating, 25–26
job searches
    resources for first, 2–3
    resumes for, 4–7
    social media and, 3–4
    successful strategies for, 3

L

leaders. *See also* administrators
    collaboration and, 70–72, 81
    communication skills and, 68–69
    empathy and, 81
    qualities of good, 80–81
    risk taking and, 100–102
leadership. *See also* administrators
    community outreach and, 85–87
    demonstrating, 79–82
    learning and, 99–100
    risk taking and, 100–102
    understanding emotions and, 83
learning, leading and, 99–100
learning curves, 37–38
    on the job, 39–41
    listening and observing for, 38–39
    mentors for, 41–42
legislative days, hosting, 55
legitimate power, 98
Less Is More (Baumbach and Miller), 76
library associations, 2
library programs
    advocacy programs for, 58–59
    preparing budgets for, 56–58
library school placement offices, 2
LinkedIn, 4, 114
listening. *See also* active listening
    administrators and, 100
    collaboration and, 81
    emotional intelligence (EI) and, 84
    leaders and, 81
literacy committees, 43

M

managers. *See* administrators
managing up, 63–65
master's degrees, grants and scholarships for, 51–52
Mayer, John, 82
meetings, administrators and, 104–105
mentors, finding, 41–42
Miller, Linda L., 76
multiple job offers, 27–28

N

National Board Certification of Teachers, 84–85
National Education Association (NEA), professional development publications, 50
networking, 114, 115
New on the Job: A School Library Media Specialist's Guide (Toor and Weisburg), 4
newspapers, as source for first jobs, 2

O

observation, active, 39
    emotional intelligence (EI) and, 84
on the job experience, gaining, 43–44
on the job learning, 39–41
    from administrators, 40
    finding mentors for, 41–42
online courses, for professional development, 49
online teaching, 117
oral communication skills, 69
outfits, interview, 14

P

Parent Outreach Toolkit, 59
parental involvement, 35
parochial schools, employment in, 35–36
part-time employment, 30–31
pencil metaphor, 102
personal learning networks (PLNs), 106–107
perspectives, broadening, administrators and, 106–107
placement offices, library school's, as resource for first jobs, 2
Plaxo, 4
power, types of, 97–98
presentations
    at conferences, 72–74
    writing proposals for, 73
private schools, employment in, 35–36
professional associations, listing, on resumes, 6

INDEX

professional development
    conferences for, 49–50
    district, 47–48
    in-house, 48
    master's degrees for, 51–52
    online courses for, 49
    reading for, 50–51
    self-taught, 49–51
    webinars for, 49
project planning skills, improving, 75–77
proposals, writing, for conference presentations, 73
prospective employers, researching, 7–9
public librarianship, 118–119

Q

questions. *See* interview questions

R

Rasmussen, Harriette Thurber, 100
reading, for professional development, 50–51
reentering the job marketing, 114–116
references
    for resumes, 6
    selecting, 20–21
referent power, 98
relationships, collaboration skills and, 70–71
relocating to other jobs, 113–114
research, for prospective employers, 7–9
resignations, considerations for, 111–113
resources, for first jobs, 2–3
resumes
    cover letters for, 9–10
    fonts for, 5
    format, 5–6
    length for, 6
    listing professional associations, 6
    perfecting, 7
    printing, 5
    rebuilding, for administrative positions, 96–97
    references for, 6, 20–21
    sending, via e-mail, 6–7
    using school career centers for writing, 6
    writing, 4–5
retirement, 119–120
reward power, 98
risk taking, leadership and, 100–102

S

salary negotiation, 28–30
Salovey, Peter, 82

scholarships, for master's degrees, 51
school librarians
    career changes and, 117–118
    collaboration and, 70–72
School Library Program and Health and Wellness Toolkit, 59
secondary school library positions, interview questions for, 15
self-taught professional development, 49–51
short-term positions, 32–33
social media, removing damaging material from, 3–4
social networking, value of, 4
speech hesitations, 69
staff development. *See* professional development
state library associations, as resource for first jobs, 2
substituting, 33–34

T

teaching, at graduate schools, 116–117
team players, 59
    becoming, 65–68
    managing up and, 64
technology planning committees, 43
telephone interviews, 19–20
tenure, earning, 44–46
thank-you notes, 22
toolkits, for advocacy programs, 59
Toor, Ruth, 4

V

vendor advisory boards, 87–89
volunteering, reentering job market and, 115–116

W

wait times, effective use of, 22
web pages, creating, for job searches, 2
webinars
    for professional development, 49
    for reentering job market, 115
work environments
    creating, in new districts, 107–108
    creating positive, administrators and, 107–108
    emotional intelligence (EI) and, 107–108
workshops, for professional development, 48–49

Y

Young Adult Library Services Association, 118

www.ingramcontent.com/pod-product-compliance
Lightning Source LLC
Chambersburg PA
CBHW071412300426
44114CB00016B/2281